To James &
God He
loves you
Harley & Mann[...]

Joshua 1:9   N.   Psalms 37: 3-5

SOVIET UNION

ARCTIC CIRCLE

CHUKCHI SEA

NOATAK RIVER

NOATAK

KOBUK RIVER
KIANA   AMBLER
KOTZEBUE   KOBUK
BALDWIN PENINSULA   NOORVIK   SHUNGNAK
KOTZEBUE   SELAWIK
SOUND   SELAWIK RIVER

SOVIET UNION
UNITED STATES

SEWARD PENINSULA

NOME

BERING SEA

BERING SEA

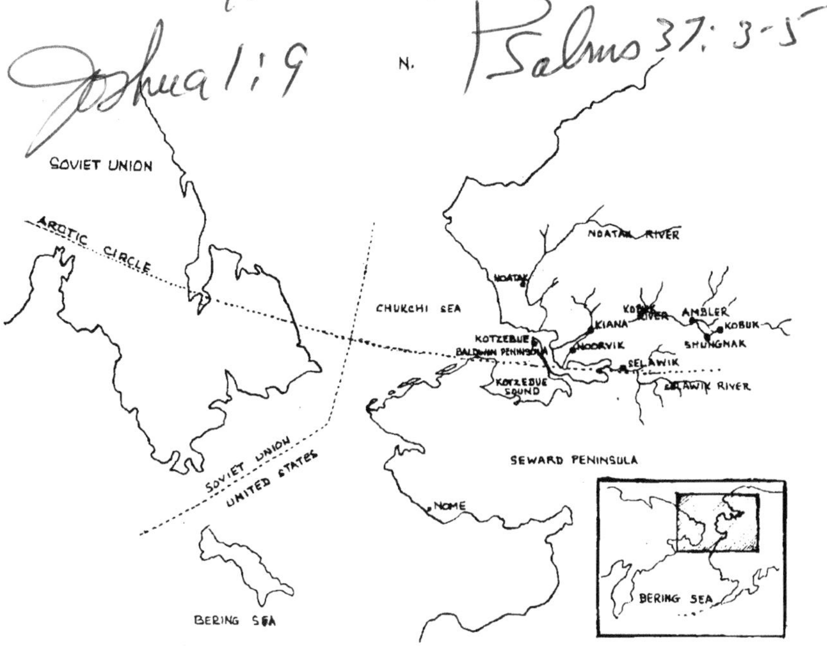

We met Harley and Martha and their family soon after their arrival in Alaska in 1966, and our trips north of the Arctic Circle ended at their home for five years. We heard their children pray to thank God they did not live in crowded LA. Boat trips with them on Kotzebue Sound and the Kobuk River with views of the magnificent Northern Lights remain precious memories. The Eskimos, knowing we were lost on the Kobuk River, lined the river banks with lanterns for a mile to show us the way home. Naomi and Bill met at the Fresno, California, Fountain of Youth center which was directed by Rolland Myers, the man who led Harley and Martha to Christ. Harley's photo with frozen eyelashes, taken after a dog-sled trip in 30-degree below zero weather, hung in a main Atlanta, Georgia, Home Mission Board hallway. Bill passed the photo each day, a constant reminder to pray. We heartily recommend this book and its story of sacrificial mission service.

Bill and Naomi Hunke, Sedona, Arizona
Executive Secretary, Alaska Baptist
Convention, 1966-1971

This book is an outgrowth of the ministry of Harley and Martha Shield to Northwest Alaska. It is a moving account of God's call and their dedicated response. It is filled with adventure, hardship, joy, and examples of their incredible faith and the miraculous works of God.

J.D. Back, Missionary
Director of Missions,
Alaska Baptist Convention, 1970-1994

Serving Christ where He leads may take many turns. When those turns lead through isolation, impoverished conditions by man's standards, and reflect nothing of a "big city pastorate," the going gets tough. The story of God's leadership in the life service of Harley and Martha Shield as they faithfully served Him is a missionary classic. To serve a lifetime in Arctic missions requires the same stuff that sent Carey to India and Judson to Burma. The Shields lived for the Lord in their corner of the world with the love, joy, and tears that make missionary stories tug at our hearts and demand our dedication—and did it well. Across their lives is surely stamped God's approval of "Well done, my good and faithful servants."

Edward G. Medaris
Lifetime Alaska Baptist Pastor and Journalist

Loud Singer and Little Bird

Nipilaaq and Ukillaq
(Nip' a Laak) and (Oo keel' yaak)
of the Arctic Missions

by

Harley D. and Martha Shield

ISBN 0-9664583-0-3

Library of Congress Catalog Card Number: 98-66972

Front cover photo by Daryl Ryder
Kotzebue, Alaska

Printed by
Maverick Publications • P.O. Box 5007 • Bend, Oregon 97708

The Shield Family

Martha Jean Ellenwood Shield, born 12/30/28
in Pacific Grove, CA.,

Married Harley D. Shield 8/31/47
in Santa Barbara, CA.

Harley Dixon Shield, born 5/13/23, in Anaheim, CA.

Their children:

Bonnie Jean, born 12/02/48 in San Jose, CA.

Ted Lee, born 2/27/50 in San Jose, CA.

Lou Ann, born 3/3/53 in San Jose, CA.

Larry Richard, born 07/09/55 in Hoopa, CA.
Went to be with the Lord 9/25/82

Danny Dixon, born 2/15/57 in Hoopa, CA.

Timothy Allen, born 8/24/59 in Hoopa, CA.

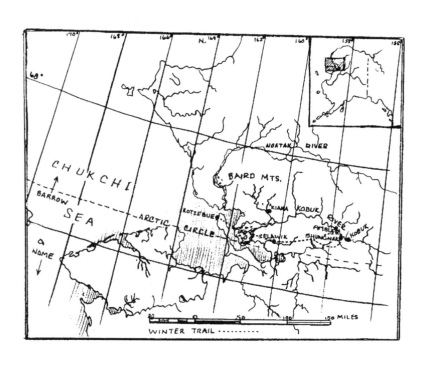

Shields' Missions and Planes

Arctic missions they have served:

Kotzebue

Shungnak

Ambler

Selawik

Kiana

Kobuk

Airplanes they have used:

1972 to 1976, a 1947 rag-wing Cessna 170

1976 to 1978, a 1953 Cessna 180

1978 to 1981, a Cessna 206

1981 to 1986, a Piper PA 28 - 180 D

1986 to 1994, a Piper 32-260 (Cherokee 6)

Dedication

To cousin Janet for her vision, dedication,
and untiring efforts in making this book possible
and to Darlene for her delightful sketches

Introduction

Life in the arctic is interesting and exciting! We are never sure what the weather will do, so many times I just go up in our plane and look around. Kotzebue used to be the polar bear hunting capital of the world, but so many hunters have killed them that hunting with planes or motorized equipment is now forbidden. There are also many other animals living on the tundra and in the low willow trees and in the many lakes.

If we had known we were to live with the Eskimos for over 20 years, I am sure we would have tried to learn the language when we first came here. We waited several years before starting, and found it was difficult because inflections in one's voice can cause differences in meanings. But we now use Eskimo singing regularly, both with the Eskimos in our churches and on our weekly radio program in Kotzebue. In each radio broadcast we include several English songs and several English hymns that have been translated into Eskimo, along with a message in English.

I was born and grew up in Southern California, and Martha was born and raised in the San Francisco Bay area. After we were married and had three of our six children, we turned our lives completely over to the Lord, and although we have had many trials we have been richly rewarded and our every need has been provided for. We started a Baptist Church among the Hoopa Indians in Northern California and we started one of our four missions with the Eskimos above the Arctic Circle. All are growing in the Lord. We meet weekly with our Arctic mission churches and share experiences and our love of the Lord Jesus Christ.

In order to reach all the churches in one week it requires 400 to 600 miles of travel! So it is necessary to use our airplane. When we first started we only had snowmobiles to use in winter and boats in the summer. We also used commercial bush flights. It was rough going and took considerable time. Now that we have our own plane it is quicker and easier, as long as the weather permits. We pile everything we will need for a few days in the plane and take off. The plane is also very useful in hauling building materials and camp supplies when needed.

Landing at the small town's airstrip (we used to have a plane with skiis and land on the rivers or snow in the winter, before the oil money permitted improvement of the airstrips), we go to the local church, where we live while we are in that town. If the oil stove has not been lit we start it up and get ready for services.

The local residents arrive for church bundled up in their parkas and fur lined (or modern insulation lately) trousers and boots. They are usually cheerful and happy, and we greet each other, share experiences since last we met, and have our church services. Martha plays the piano, or pump organ. I play the guitar and preach, and we both sing. We use the guitar when singing the Eskimo translated songs. I am a loud singer, so loud, in fact, that an Eskimo named me Nipalaaq (Nip' a laak), meaning loud or noisy.

The Eskimos don't always give a name because of its meaning. More often it is given in memory of some other person or relative. Nipalaaq was a well liked Eskimo preacher of a generation ago.

In the same way Martha was given the name of Ukillaq (Oo keel' yaak) which is the name of small bird with a cry that sounds like its name. It was given to Martha by a sweet old Christian lady because it was her grandmother's name. Thus we have our Eskimo names, Nipalaaq and Ukillaq.

Harley D. Shield
Kotzebue, Alaska

Prologue

I put my hand on the radio, bowed my head, and silently prayed, "Jesus, I want you to come into my heart."

I had just responded to Billy Graham's invitation to accept Jesus. His evangelistic crusade was being broadcast over the radio, and had reached out to the wild, forested mountains of Northern California, and into my receptive heart.

For perhaps the first time in my life I had listened to a Christian program in its entirety. I was a new industrial arts teacher in the High School on the Hoopa Indian Reservation. It was a Sunday afternoon, March 1954, and I was idly twisting the radio dial, searching for some program to listen to.

For a reason known to God, Billy's sermon caught my interest. I do not recall the contents of his message, but I do remember responding to the invitation.

I thought, "This is a good thing to do," and obediently accepted his challenge.

The program was over and I turned the dial to some popular music, and thought no more about it.

It may seem strange to some people, but this event was the opening chapter of a whole new way of life, because one week later, Martha and I were invited to attend a revival meeting at the Hoopa Presbyterian Church.

1.

We Meet the Lord

*I did not know why we were going to church. I thought
it was because we decided our children, Bonnie, aged
five, and Ted, aged four, needed to learn about the
Bible.*

I was teaching school on the Hoopa Indian Reservation in
Northern California. Although the natives offered to take our
children to Sunday School at the Hoopa Presbyterian Indian
Mission, we decided to take them there ourselves.

Then, in the spring of 1954, a revival was held. I again
wondered why we were going there. The pastor of the church
had invited a Conservative Baptist minister from Oregon to hold
the services.

Pastor Roland Meyer was not only a good speaker, but he
played the accordion and trumpet, and sang well too.

Now I decided it was the music that was drawing us to church. I played the guitar a little at that time, and we both loved to hear good music, and I have always enjoyed music, myself.

After a few nights of his services, I believe it was the music that drew Martha to go forward and accept Christ as her Savior. I think it was the song he sang, "It's in My heart", that captured her attention.

I went forward with her, just to keep her company. I was glad she had found something that pleased her so much.

She told me later that she went forward because he was so happy and she wanted some of that happiness, too.

The next night at the service, something happened to me. I suddenly became acutely aware of the message. I listened with the kind of attention that makes one forget everything else. He was talking about the time Jesus was led away from Gethsemane by the soldiers, and all His disciples deserted Him. However, Peter followed from afar off.

The thrust of his sermon was that we in the congregation might be like Peter, who believe in Jesus and His promises, but we are actually standing in the shadows, afar off, rather than being alongside Him.

For the first time I saw Jesus as a real person, and not just some vague Biblical character that I generally believed in. I agreed with the logic of the sermon that if Jesus is alive and real, I should be along side Him, and not like Peter standing afar off.

At the close of the sermon Brother Meyer asked the question, "Is there anyone here who will follow Jesus?"

It was then that I spoke out loudly, oblivious to everyone, "I will!"

Martha and I were sitting close to the wall at the end of the pew, and as I turned to make my way to the aisle, I could see all heads turn toward me and the people falling back to let me by.

I can only remember one other time that I listened with such attention to a pastor. I was 12 years old attending an Episcopal church with some friends, and when the pastor asked one of those rhetorical questions, I answered out loudly, "yes" to the amusement of everyone present.

I made my way forward and a very strange thing happened that night. They did not talk to me or pray with me as they had with Martha the night before. As I think back on it, I believe they thought I was already a Christian and just rededicating my life. At any rate, something happened to me inside.

In the following days for the first time I began listening to Christian music on the radio. The second thing I noticed was that as we started attending church regularly, I began hearing and understanding the pastor's messages.

He had always mentioned sin in man's life and the necessity of repentance and receiving Jesus Christ as the means of salvation from our sins. As the truth of these messages began to sink in, I realized I hadn't prayed these prayers of repentance and accepting Christ as the means of salvation from our sins. I began to wonder if I was really saved or not.

So, one evening when I was alone in the church, I said to myself, "I'll just kneel down here and pray and ask God to cleanse me from my sins." I asked Jesus to come into my life, and I promised to follow Him.

Now as I look back on it, I know I was saved the moment I said, "I will," but it didn't hurt me a bit to go through the steps and make sure.

It's like an evangelist told our daughter, Bonnie, at a revival meeting when she was 9 years old. She had come forward and said she did not know whether she was saved or not. He said, "We can always pray again and make sure. If you're starting out on a long trip and don't know how much gasoline is in your tank, it doesn't hurt to fill it up."

Martha and I were both saved within 24 hours of each other. It happened to both of us on the mission field. We both started teaching Sunday School the following week. We began our service with the Indian people in California, and we have been working with them and the Eskimo people ever since.

Now I know why we were attending the Hoopa Indian Mission. God was calling to us, and when God calls, you come! But we had no idea of the interesting and exciting things He had planned for our future.

2.

God Knows the Future

by Martha

When we turned our lives over to Christ, the Lord started taking control. We did not always realize this. Sometimes we would feel He had deserted us.

I especially remember the time about a year later, when we had an opportunity to attend a Bible conference at Mt. Hermon, California. Another Christian family was going with us. We were thrilled and excited!

First we drove to Santa Barbara, CA. to spend a week with my parents. Then we were going to join our friends and go on to the conference.

A couple of days before we were to leave my folks, Ted broke out with the mumps on one side of his neck. We had three children by then, (Lou Ann was born the year before) and our friends had three. We did not dare chance having our other children and theirs come down with mumps, so we could not take them. Mom was not well enough to take care of three children, so I did not get to go.

It really did not seem fair. Here I had given my life to the Lord. I was trying hard to please Him. Now when I was trying to learn more about Him, He would not let me go to the meeting!

Harley went on with our friends. I stayed for another week with my parents. I was able to sew some new clothes for my mom, and we had a good two-weeks-visit together.

I still did not understand why God had allowed the mumps at that time. Ted never got it on the other side and none of our other children caught them, and I had missed an inspiring Bible conference.

Because of Harley's schooling and the expense of raising all our children, we were not able financially to go back to Santa Barbara for a long time. In fact, it was three years later, and babies Larry and Danny had joined us. Mom was in the hospital, dying. I saw her for a short 15 minutes. She needed rest, so we planned to come back later. But she went into a coma and died that night.

As I look back now, I treasure those two weeks the Lord gave me with Mom. He knew what was ahead!

This was only the beginning of our lives as we served God His way, and were rewarded with blessings.

3.

Going to Bible School

As we continued to work in the Presbyterian church,
we met several traveling evangelists who lived by
faith for their livelihood.

This idea intrigued us. I had felt the need for more Bible training, but did not feel we could live without my steady salary. Could I really quit work and devote my time entirely to study?

We decided to trust in the Lord, and I enrolled at Multnomah School of the Bible in Portland, Oregon. It was a special one-year "grad" course, designed for people who wanted a year of concentrated Bible study.

We told the people of the church that we were going to try this Bible and see if it really worked. We were not going to tell any one when we had need of either money or food. I had read the life of Hudson Taylor, the founder of China Inland Missions. His spiritual secret was "to move man by God, through prayer alone." Therefore, Martha and I elected to follow his path.

At the end of the school year in June, I, of course, had no employment and we had to move out of the school housing. Since we had no money to go to Bible School, I accepted an offer to work for the summer as a marker for two loggers in the area. A marker is one who measures off the logs after they are felled, into 40' lengths, or whatever length they choose, so the buckers (those who cut the logs in lengths) won't have to waste time measuring. I had worked at this the previous summer.

We stored a lot of our household goods with some friends in Hoopa, took our tent and camping gear and moved out to the Bluff Creek camp grounds on the Klamath River, about 40 miles from Hoopa. We continued to attend church and serve the Lord in various ways from this home base while waiting for the loggers to start me to work.

However, after about 2 weeks, they came by and said there would be no job because of changing events. We continued camping and praying and waiting on the Lord. Little Larry was about 4 weeks old at this time, which is pretty young to be living in a tent in the wilderness. Martha would have to get up for the 2 a.m. feeding, light the Coleman lamp to try to keep warm, while she nursed the baby.

Actually, in spite of the cool nights, we had a good time. The kids went swimming every day. We went hiking. We took our old jeep up some scary mountain roads. Back of our minds, however, we were wondering how the Lord was going to get us to Bible school.

We continued camping for another two weeks and then the Burtons, a Christian family, came and offered us the use of their house until the school year started. Sam Burton was a teacher at the Hoopa Elementary School and they were going on a trip for a few weeks. They thought it would be nice if we wanted to live in their house until they came back.

We felt very grateful to them and to the Lord, and accepted immediately. We still didn't have any money to go to school, and I couldn't find any employment, so we waited and waited.

The teachers came back at the end of August and we remained with them for a few more days. Then we received a check in the mail for $292.00 with a note, with the explanation that some of our Christian friends had gathered this money together to send us off to Bible school.

Back in 1954, $292.00 would be about a month's salary, so we immediately began packing for the great adventure. When I resigned my teaching position, I had applied to withdraw my retirement contributions, which would amount to $350.00. We did not receive this check until almost Thanksgiving, so we were not able to use that money to move to Portland.

One of the Indian families in Hoopa gave us five large salmon that they had caught in the river. So Martha, with their help, canned 75 quarts of salmon. We then had a little money, a lot of salmon, four children, and a lot of faith. And as Paul said in Acts, "We loosed from Troas and set sail for Macedonia," which we did, so to speak.

Completing our equipment for the adventure was the song "Mansion over a Hilltop," and the Bible verse from Philippians 4:19 "But my God shall supply all your need, according to His riches in glory by Christ Jesus."

Everyone who sets out on a mission for the Lord Jesus Christ ought to have a Bible verse and a song. The verse keeps you going through the hard times and the song cheers you up during the discouraged times.

We rented a trailer, loaded it with our meager belongings and attached it to our 1949 Dodge. Then we were off to Portland, Oregon.

When we arrived at Portland, we had to find a place to rent pretty quickly. It's not very pleasant to run around in a strange city with four children to care for, a short money supply, and no place to live. The Lord led us to an economical apartment over a garage, and then a month later, Peter Scruggs, the business manager for Multnomah School of the Bible, rented us his old family home for $50.00 a month. It was a two story Victorian house, and we remained there for the following year.

4.

The Year of Testing

One Monday morning while I was at school, one of the men of our church knocked on our door. He was a little embarrassed, but He asked Martha if Ted needed a new pair of shoes. He said his wife, who was Ted's Sunday school teacher, noticed that Ted kept his boots on while all the other children had theirs off.

Martha had to admit that six-year-old Ted's shoes were worn out. (In fact the soles were flapping.) This man said, "I'm a new Christian and I've never done this before, but I'd like to buy Ted a new pair of shoes."

We certainly praised the Lord that night for His watchful care over our little children.

The year at Multnomah was surely a test of our faith and a wonderful show of God's supply and grace. This year was what is called a "Red Sea Experience." This means that as Moses and the children of Israel faced the Red Sea with the Pharaoh's armies closing in behind, and impassable countries on both right and left, they had nowhere to go but to the Lord.

This is when you find out whether God will deliver or not. I believe this type of experience is absolutely necessary for anyone contemplating mission work for Jesus.

If you do not have the knowledge burned deep within your soul that Jesus will truly never leave you nor forsake you, you will be easy prey for Satan.

Martha and I cannot really remember how God took care of our needs day after day. At first I did not feel led to find work, as I was busy studying. One time Martha did persuade me to go pick plums across the river in Washington State. I worked all one rainy day for a few cents, ran out of gas on the way home, and had to trade my electric drill for a couple of gallons to get home.

Towards the middle of the year I began to work at the school four hours a day for $1.00 an hour. Every month I would get about $80.00. We paid $50.00 a month for rent, a few dollars for electricity, water and gas, bought about 10- gallons of stove oil for the furnace, and Martha would go to the grocery store with about 5 or 6 dollars for groceries. We had lots of biscuits that year and nothing very fancy, but we really never went hungry, either. We knew God was really testing us for future adventures, so we did not complain. We never did tell people of the church, or any one else, of our needs. But somehow, through the spring months, people began to get the idea and helped us in different ways.

Another expression of God's care happened shortly after we moved to Portland. Little Larry, by now about 3 months old, had developed a cold from our camping experience and was beginning to sound real bad with his wheezing and hard breathing. We were absolutely broke and had no money for a doctor and did not really want to go to the county for help. But we knew that unless something changed for the better, we would have to do just that.

We knelt by Larry's little form that night and told the Lord that we needed His help, that Larry was very sick, and if he was not better in the morning, we would have to search for public health care.

We really praised the Lord the next morning when Larry began to improve, and within few days was breathing quite normally.

The mother of one of our Hoopa friends lived in Portland, and she asked Martha to give her a permanent. She wanted to pay Martha, but Martha refused the money. The lady said, "By the way, I have a lot of vegetables from my garden in the car. Would you like them?" Martha did not turn down the vegetables.

Another time this dear lady, whose husband was diabetic and could not eat fat asked Martha if she could use a lot of bacon grease that she had saved from frying her husband's bacon. Martha said, "yes, yes," and for a long time we had plenty of bacon grease to mix with our biscuits that Martha baked.

That evening as we sat down to our meal of "pulse and water" so to speak, we pulled a scripture from our little box called the "Bread of Life." The scripture said, "Better is a dinner of herbs where love is, than a stalled ox and hatred therewith."

One of the hardest tests for us that winter was the time we got an urgent call from Martha's father in Santa Barbara. Martha's mother was seriously ill, and he wanted her to come to visit her. We had absolutely no money, and if we were to drive down there it would mean dropping out of school and giving it up for the year.

We earnestly prayed about it and the Lord gave us this reasoning: We came to school to get Bible training, to test the Lord's Word and promises and definitely felt it was of the Lord's leading. Very sorrowfully and regretfully we had to let her father know that we couldn't come.

Martha's mother was a very fine Christian woman, who was excited about Martha's serving the Lord, and we felt that she would understand. We weren't too sure about her father's understanding of the situation, but we had to take that chance. Only time and eternity will tell us the results of that decision.

Our Christmas, however, was one of the best we have experienced. About two weeks before the Christmas season, Martha attended a Women's fellowship at the Bible school. While visiting with one of the student's wives, Martha mentioned that she hadn't any toys for the children and went on talking of other things. Two weeks went by and the day before Christmas, we had a pretty bare house. Bonnie had asked Martha what she would like to have for Christmas, and Martha replied, "I would like to see this dining room table loaded with food."

Late that afternoon there was a knock at the door and a young man asked Martha, "Is this where the Harley Shields live?"

Martha said "Yes." The young man explained that his wife was the one that Martha was talking to at the Multnomah fellowship, and he was pastoring a small church on the Washington side of the Columbia River. Their church had chosen us as their Christmas family. Then he went out to his car and began to bring in box after box of food. After the young man had left, Bonnie told Martha, "You got what you wanted, didn't you, Mommy?"

As we sat down to Christmas dinner the next day, we truly had much to be thankful for, as we celebrated our Lord's birth.

One advantage to not having a lot of fancy food, is that your children learn to appreciate most any kind of food. We were invited to breakfast by one of our church families and Bonnie, Ted, and Lou Ann were eating fried eggs as fast as the lady could cook them. The kind lady mentioned that she wished her children would eat eggs like that. Martha and I glanced at each other with a knowing smile and kept our secret.

By the time spring had rolled around, some of the church members knew that we were truly living by faith and would come and check on us once in a while. A young husband used to come and say, "I'm going to look in your cupboards and see if you have any food. No use to ask how you are doing, you'll just say 'Fine.'"

Another time, the pastor dropped by to see if we could use some meat. Martha said, "Yes, but we don't have a refrigerator." The pastor had a hard time believing this, so went out in the kitchen to look for himself. Without saying anything, he went out and rented a refrigerator for us for the remainder of the school year.

As I mentioned earlier, we don't really know how God met all our needs, but he surely did through all these experiences and many more.

One of the most forlorn sounds I have ever heard was pouring a 5 gallon can of stove oil, all I could afford, into an empty 500 gallon underground tank.

This adventure may sound foolish and very dangerous, but the successful completion of that year set the tone for the rest of our spiritual life and journey with the Lord Jesus Christ.

5.

We Begin Preaching and Teaching

*"I sure don't like running my log truck on the road
when it's time for the school bus to be delivering our
kids home!" The burly truck driver was referring to
the new school bus route down the Klamath River. I
was the bus driver, and it scared me, too!*

It all began after our summer of 1956 in Portland, Oregon.
The school year was over and things had begun to look better. I
spent the summer supervising the work students did on some of
the buildings at Multnomah.

In spite of our poverty, we had gathered up more possessions
than we came to Portland with. Now, when we felt the Lord was
calling us back to Hoopa, we had a problem of how to get our
belongings there.

We loaded a home-made trailer precariously heavy and
headed south, stopping at the farm of a close relative near Salem,

Oregon. We spent several days there, working on the trailer and car and relaxing.

Because of the high temperatures in the Willamette Valley, and our heavily loaded trailer, I was worried about the tires giving way. So we elected to cross over the coast range to the coast highway and followed the cooler route down to northern California.

After finally arriving at Hoopa safely, we rented a house and I began looking for some kind of work. I was not interested in teaching school, but a young teacher who had been employed to teach in a 1-room school in Martins Ferry on the Klamath River, had not received her certificate from the state. Since I had a teaching certificate, they asked me to work with her to satisfy the State's requirement. She expected her certificate to come within the month.

While I was engaged in this occupation, the school district closed a 1-room school at Morek, about 30 miles down river from Hoopa, and about 15 miles from Martin's Ferry because they could not keep a teacher there.

They asked me if I would be interested in moving to Morek and drive a school bus, bringing those elementary students to Martin's Ferry as well as picking up several high school students and delivering them to Weitchpec. This is a little community at the confluence of the Klamath and Trinity Rivers. The road to Weitchpec joined with the Orleans-Hoopa highway at this point. There the high school students would be picked up by the bus from Orleans and taken on to the high school in Hoopa. In the late afternoon this process would be reversed.

The 1-room school house at Morek consisted of one big class room, and a small kitchen and dining room, as they had a hot lunch program in all these little schools. The building was heated by propane gas and there was a small light plant that ran on propane. The school would supply the gas and the building would be rent free.

Martha and I decided that I would take the job and we would move to Morek. Morek is deep in wilderness country, with a dirt road only 1 1/2 lanes wide carved into the hillside, sometimes as much as 200' above the river.

The road was also heavily used by logging trucks during the day. This made driving the school bus rather exciting. I learned later that the truck drivers were scared to death of the potential for trouble with a fat school bus. They kind of quit driving about the time the bus was supposed to be traveling.

So, Martha and I and our four children moved into the school house in Morek, and I began my career as a school bus driver. After the teacher got her certificate, I worked during the day at maintenance at the Martin's Ferry school, and I no longer had to help her to teach.

There was plenty to do not only at the school, but at our home. There was gravity flow water, light plants, and a multitude of other duties that people who live in the woods find to occupy their time.

The first thing Martha and I began to miss was the church fellowship. There was no church in the area and the Indian families lived about a mile apart along the road on the little land claims, so it was kind of lonely.

One week end, about 2 weeks after we had moved down, we decided to drive to Eureka, about 85 miles over winding mountain roads, just to go to church. As far as we knew, that was the nearest Southern Baptist church.

We visited Calvary Baptist church, more through providence than by chance. George Kendall, the area missionary for our Baptist churches, was attending the church that night. We met him and shared our experiences and where we were. Being a good church planter and missionary, he said, "I'll be up to visit you next week."

He encouraged us to start a little mission Sunday school in the area to see if we could minister not only to ourselves, but to the people living in the area. George left us, wishing us well and promising to pray for us and we began looking for a building we could use for a meeting house.

There was a small sawmill a mile or two down the road from the school house, with a few people still working in it. We also found an empty 20' x 32' building. When we learned this building belonged to an Indian family in Hoopa, we asked and were given permission to use it for church meetings. We also learned that a small Indian mission at Pecwan, 20 miles down the river at the end of the road, had used the building for meetings off and on.

We drove down and talked to the pastor and he readily assented to having us take over the spiritual responsibilities in that area. So Morek Baptist Mission was born, and I preached my very first sermon the following Sunday

It was a good thing we had a fairly large family during the following year, for they comprised most of the services. I would teach the adult class and Martha would teach all the children we were able to gather together. The difficult part for her was teaching her own children, as the older boys many times felt they had to show that they were not as religious as their parents and would act accordingly.

However, these were learning years. We were enthusiastic and really enjoyed what we were doing. We faithfully went down to the building for Wednesday night prayer meeting, and to my remembrance, not one of local people ever attended the week night services. However, we gathered our little family together with a Coleman lamp for light, and had a great time, singing and praying together.

The little mission continued as long as we were there and we were able to help some people through the next two years that we ministered there.

6.

Almost Twins

by Martha

Valentine's Day was to be very special because we were expecting our fifth child that day. The only problem was that Harley was driving a school bus in Northern California. I was alone in Morek with my children thirty six miles down a snaky mountain road from my doctor at the Indian Reservation in Hoopa.

Worried, I decided to drive our car with the four children over the mud and gravel road to Hoopa and stay with friends. Chuck and Maxine Lee only had a two-room house, but they were willing to let us stay there to await the baby. Maxine was also expecting a baby in about 3 weeks or so.

When the doctor came and checked over my situation, he decided to remain in Hoopa, although he had planned to go 80 miles away to Eureka to attend a meeting.

Fortunately, for my peace of mind, Harley had to return to Hoopa to get the bus repaired, so he was there to reassure me.

As usual, babies have minds of their own, and nothing seemed to be happening. That night, Maxine and Chuck slept in the front room, along with their daughter and our four kids. They gave Harley and me their bedroom.

Around midnight, Chuck stuck his head in the bedroom and asked if I was going to be calling the doctor pretty soon. I said, "Oh, I don't know —."

He said, "If you're not, Maxine is." We had forgotten Maxine had had her previous child one month early. Since there was no telephone, Chuck went to get the doctor.

When Chuck got there, the doctor asked, "Is Martha ready?"

And Chuck said, "No, but Maxine is."

So the doctor and the nurse came to the house and they also brought a small oxygen tent with them. They always brought one when they made home deliveries, just as a preventative measure.

Harley and I crawled out of bed and Maxine crawled in. The doctor got there just in time to deliver her baby. Then she crawled out of bed, and I crawled in and had mine. Maxine and I always said, "It took two of us to have twins!"

Her baby was not breathing properly, so the doctor put it in the little oxygen tent. Within a couple of hours the baby and the nurse were flown to a hospital in Eureka. After an examination, they found that one kidney had to be removed by surgery. The baby, now named Bruce, survived and did fine. Danny, our baby, was fine.

We have thought over this experience many times, realizing God's care for both Maxine and me. If I had had the doctor "down river." he could not have been with Maxine. If she had had the doctor at her home in Hoopa, I could not have had him at my home in Morek.

Danny and Bruce have both grown up to be fine young men and fathers. Although they have never met, perhaps in God's timing, "the twins" may some day get together again.

7.

Danny's Surgery

by Martha

I was rather nervous as I guided the car around the sharp, narrow curves along the Klamath River. The road clung to the mountainside about 200 feet above the river, and I didn't like the way the cliffs dropped straight down to the rushing water!

Danny was only 1 1/2 years old, but he had developed a hernia that kept appearing and then disappearing by the time I got him to a doctor. Although the doctor had not yet seen it, he said it could be dangerous or even fatal if it became strangulated. So I was determined to reach the doctor quickly this time.

I was very concerned when I went into the office to find a stranger, as my doctor was on vacation. Again the hernia had gone back inside, so this doctor did not see it either. He did not think we should wait around, but should take Danny to Eureka for surgery. When I told him we did not know a doctor, he named one, and we made an appointment.

I drove the 120 miles to Eureka, where Harley, who had been going to summer school there, met me and we discussed the problem with the surgeon. Although the surgeon did not see the hernia either, he sensed I was not one who ran to a doctor for every little thing. He felt he should go ahead and operate and check out the situation.

He assured us that it was a simple procedure. We should put Danny in the hospital the night before the surgery. He would operate early the next morning, and I could take him home in the afternoon. Harley and I agreed to the plan.

The doctor then told us he charges teachers and preachers only half of his usual fee. Since Harley was BOTH he would not charge us anything! What a surprise! We had never seen the man before - God was at work!

God does supply every need in His own wonderful way! He is so faithful.

8.

The Lord Leads Me to Seminary

"Well, Martha, we just spent $40.00 for one night in a motel. We have only $120.00 left. We must find a house to rent tomorrow, or we won't have enough for the first month's rent."

That is what happened when we stepped out in faith so I could go to seminary. Things can get a little frightening.

Actually, things had been going quite well. I had a good job, we lived in a comfortable house, but we felt we should leave all this and I should continue my Bible studies.

The school year of 1958-59 found me teaching school again. I was principal/teacher of a two-teacher school at Pecwan Elementary School, deep in the Klamath river territory. I was teaching 4th through 8th grades. Martha and I had moved our family into the principal's house on the school grounds. We had five children at this time and so the house was full.

This was a rather pleasant year for teaching as the two 8th graders were well behaved kids (a boy and a girl), and the rest of the students behaved in a better than average fashion. The kindergarten primary teacher was a fine, experienced woman, and we got along well.

During the summer before we moved to Pecwan, we had met some Baptists in Hoopa who desired to start a church, and wanted me to lead them. Still young and full of energy, Martha and I agreed. We began our little mission with a vacation Bible school under a walnut tree, at the home of one of the prospective members.

During the winter we were able to rent a small building for our little church.

Then on Sunday morning Martha and I would load our children into the car at Pecwan, with food for lunch, and drive the 30 miles through rain and snow to Hoopa. There we would have Sunday School and church service, and when the weather was good, have a picnic lunch somewhere. We would remain all day until the evening church service was over at about 8:30 p.m. After that, we would take the hour's drive back to Pecwan.

We still kept the Morek mission going by driving up on Tuesday evenings. We would pick up people for evening Bible study and preaching service, then drive the 15 miles back to Pecwan.

We continued this schedule through the winter.

Towards the end of the school year I began to notice the wear and tear on my mind. Friday night, after the school week, I would be turning off the children and school work and trying to turn on the church work and the different people involved. Sunday night, driving home from the church service at Hoopa, I would find myself trying to turn off 'church' and turning my mind back to the school children and all that it involved.

I soon became convinced that I needed to make a choice, either cut way back on the spiritual work and concentrate on school teaching, or turn my back on school teaching and go to a

Seminary for training and apply to our Home mission Board for an appointment as missionaries.

After praying about this for some time, Martha and I decided to take the latter course, and I did not renew my teaching contract for the school year of 1959-60.

Once again I resigned from the teaching profession. We moved to Hoopa and rented a little shack. We purchased a gallon of Chlorox and washed the place with a garden hose and a mixture of chlorox and water. When we moved into this little hot house, Martha was expecting our 6th and last child. I wasn't able to find any employment, but did manage to lead the Hoopa congregation to pay me $5.00 a month for gasoline. By now it had been organized into the Hoopa First Baptist Church.

We also had a young college student as a summer worker and we spent the summer chasing up and down mountain roads, visiting the widely scattered families, seeking to lead them to Christ.

Towards the end of the summer, we were able to lead one lady to faith in Jesus Christ in a little mountain cabin above the Klamath River.

Don Courtney, the young summer worker, who is now a foreign missionary in Guatemala, made the remark, as we left this little cabin, "After chasing all over the mountains this summer, I have learned the value of one soul."

In August, our last child, Timothy, was born, while I was pastor in our association-wide youth camp, which was fortunately held in a nearby Boy Scout camp. The baby was a home delivery, as were the other two boys born in Hoopa, and I was able to get home to Martha shortly after Tim's birth.

A church member volunteered to stay with Martha the remaining days of my camp duties and I was able to return to camp. The camp missionary at this time was a young Cuban seminary student by the name of Raphael De Armas. I shared with him my desire to enroll at Golden Gate Baptist Theological

Seminary which had just moved into its new campus in Marin County on the San Francisco Bay.

Raphael encouraged me and told me to look him up when I got there.

The testing of my faith was getting stronger as the deadline for enrolling approached, as I had absolutely no financial means to attend school. I also had a family of six children and a faithful wife to take care of. Finally the last few days came, and not willing to give up, I decided to drive the 350 miles to Golden Gate and see if the Lord could get me in.

My total financial assets as I started this journey were $5.00 and a Standard Oil credit card.

Upon arriving at the seminary, I went in to see the business manager. He advised that I would need at least $85.00 for books and insurance in order to enroll. He told me I should go back home and work and save up some money.

Martha's uncle, a Pentecostal preacher, lived in Salinas, about 80 miles south of San Francisco. I decided to go down and see if I could borrow $100.00 from him. When I arrived in Salinas I discovered that he was in the hospital recovering from a heart attack. I visited him but decided not to mention my need for money.

Returning next day to the seminary, I talked once more with the business manager, but had no success. I returned to the parking lot, sadly resigned to returning home to Hoopa. As I was getting into my car, Raphael De Armas came walking across the parking lot. After a warm greeting, I shared with him my total lack of success.

Raphael, who is an enthusiastic speaker and persuader took me by the arm and said, "Lets go back and see the business manager. I'll get you in."

And sure enough, he did!

I sat in the office as Raphael persuaded the business manager to put up half the money and he, Raphael, would guarantee the rest. Even though he didn't have any more money than I did.

I was assigned a dormitory room, and the next day I found a part-time job in a gasoline service station. For three days, I lived on peanut butter crackers, purchased from a vending machine, on a budget of 30 cents a day. After 3 days, When I figured I had some equity in the job, I asked the manager for a small salary advance, which he readily gave me.

Meanwhile, Martha was back at Hoopa awaiting word from me and looking for the check that contained my retirement funds that I had withdrawn again.

Then the people that owned the house wanted it back again, making it necessary for Martha and the children to leave. Some friends of ours bought our old Jeep for $300.00, so Martha decided to take the children and visit her sister in South San Francisco until we could find a house to rent.

Her sister had 2 children, and adding 6 more began to build up tensions rather quickly. I drove down and picked up Martha and our children, and we spent one night in a motel for $40.00, leaving us a balance of about $120.00 cash.

We knew we had to find a house the next day, or we would be in serious trouble. Someone mentioned that we should try Novato, a small community about 15 miles north of the seminary.

By the afternoon of the next day the Lord led us to a large older-style house which we were able to rent for $100.00 a month. We paid one month's rent, arranged to have the utilities turned on, and felt safe for at least a month.

Sometime during the next week, Martha was able to find employment with the Simmons Mattress Factory in San Francisco, on the night shift. We designed a plan. I would return from school shortly after noon and she would drive to San Francisco in time to start her 4 to 12 midnight shift. Then she would drive home in the wee hours of the morning, in sometimes dark and rainy weather.

At this time, I also applied for a student missions position. Our California Baptist Department of Missions had a program that would enable students to do mission work on week ends and summers for about 2/3 the regular missions salary.

Because of our previous work with the Indian people in Northern California, I was accepted, and they instructed me to make a survey and find a suitable group of natives, or a reservation on which to start a mission work.

After two weeks of research, traveling, and interviewing, we found the Round Valley Indian Reservation about 170 miles north of San Francisco that had no Baptist church.

The little town of Covelo is situated on the edge of the reservation. We visited the area and talked to folks and prayerfully decided that this would be a good place to begin work.

After getting approval from our State Mission Director, we were able to rent a house and move the family within a couple of weeks.

We had received permission from the owners of the house to have Sunday School and church meetings, and so began the Round Valley Baptist Mission. I would drive to Seminary on Monday and return on Friday evening, while it was left to Martha to hold the family together during the week.

Thus followed three years of study, visitation, church work, revivals and vacation Bible schools. This also included miles of almost empty gas tanks And very thin tires.

9.

The Shields —
Missionaries To Hoopa

"Brother Combs, how do you tell the difference between temptation and opportunity?" I had just been asked if Martha and I would like to go back to Hoopa as regularly appointed and paid Home Missionaries.

I had graduated from Golden Gate Baptist Theological Seminary in June of 1962, with a Master of Divinity degree. Martha and I were thoroughly committed to work with the North American Indians, but when we applied for this kind of work in California, there were no positions open. At that time California Southern Baptists only had three families appointed for Indian work.

One was at an Indian center in the Los Angeles area, another in Oakland, and the third, surprisingly enough, was working on the Hoopa Indian Reservation.

During our time at the seminary, our Home Mission Board had taken over the work that we had started in Hoopa, and had appointed a missionary couple there.

Brother Jack Combs, our state language missions director, said that they needed lots of workers for the Spanish people in California. Martha and I agreed to accept an appointment on this basis, and Brother Combs proceeded with the work of getting approval from our state convention and home mission board.

This normally takes a little time. During the following two weeks Martha and I felt less and less comfortable with the decision that we had made. One night about two weeks after we had talked to Brother Combs, I was so disturbed that I could not sleep. In the early morning hours, I told Martha that I believed we had made a mistake and I was going to call Brother Combs that morning.

Wouldn't you know, at 8:00 a.m. the phone rang and Brother Combs was on the line. He very cheerfully announced that the paper work had gone through and we were to be appointed as Spanish language missionaries.

I replied, "Brother Jack, you're going to hate me. We have not been comfortable with our decision, and we decided last night that we will stay with the Indian work."

He was very nice and said, "Well, just keep in touch, and God bless you."

About that time, we heard of a little Indian mission that needed a pastor in San Jose, California. We prayed about it and decided to move to San Jose and work with this little group of Indians. It was strictly volunteer work with no pay involved. So I would have to find employment.

We were able to move to San Jose, and with some difficulty, because of our six children, were able to rent a house. I found a low-paying job in the Good Will Center as the print shop manager. The next nine months were some of the most difficult of our lives. If Martha and I had ever had any hidden desire to live back in the city again, it was certainly trampled out of us in those few months.

In May of the following year, 1963, I received a phone call from Brother Combs. He was at a downtown bank on some land office business for one of the other missions, and asked if I could meet him there.

I said, "Yes, I can get off work and I'll be there in about 1/2 hour." I had no idea what he wanted, but I was certainly willing to find out.

After we extended our mutual greetings, he asked me, "How would you like to go back to Hoopa as missionaries to the Indians? Our missionary couple there has resigned."

I replied, "How do you tell the difference between opportunity and temptation? We would LOVE to go back to Hoopa!"

Martha and the family were in complete agreement with this decision, and soon we were packing to go back to Hoopa. Martha and I were both rejoicing and had a sense of deliverance as we crossed the Golden Gate Bridge late one afternoon, heading for the North country once again.

We arrived at Hoopa, found a place to live, and began our church duties. A pleasant surprise awaited us. The retiring missionary, through the help of the Home Mission Board, had secured five acres of land, right where I had always thought a Baptist church should be. And they already had a Christian construction man starting a first-unit church building.

We soon were involved with Bible School and Missionary activities in Weitchpec, Orleans, and even back to Morek, along with the church work in Hoopa.

10.

Alaska, the Land for Which We Were Prepared

My heart sank. What was I to do? The Canadian customs officer was kind but firm. "I'm sorry, sir, but you cannot cross the border and drive the Alaska Highway."

Martha and I served the Hoopa Indians from 1963 to 1966. During those years my thoughts strayed often to Alaska. The reason was, that shortly after graduating from high school in 1941, my high school buddy and I traveled to Alaska, locating in Anchorage. There I worked and played and traveled until May 1944, when I was drafted into the U. S. Army.

I took my basic training at Fort Richardson. I spent the winter on Attu Island in the Infantry, went to the lower states in the summer for advanced training, and shipped out from Wilmington, California to Calcutta, India.

We were to go up into Burma and fight the Japanese in the mud and bugs. But praise God, the Japanese surrendered seven days after we arrived in Calcutta. We remained as replacement troops until sent home in May 1946, and I was discharged in California.

I mentioned the Alaskan adventure because it will help you to understand my desire to some day return to that great land.

Now, back to our experiences in Hoopa. In early 1965 I subscribed to the Alaska Baptist Messenger, the state paper for Alaska Baptists. I figured I would start getting in tune with what was happening with Baptist work in Alaska.

I received a letter from William Hansen, the executive director of Alaska Baptists, expressing interest in my reasons for having subscribed. He asked if we would consider transferring to Kotzebue, Alaska.

I figuratively pricked up my ears, and wrote back that I was interested. The result was that the Alaska Baptist Convention and the church at Kotzebue approved our transfer. But there was a little problem with the home mission board. The last missionaries had had six children and they had not adjusted, and the missions committee did not feel it would be wise to send another large family to Kotzebue.

Of course we were all disappointed, but since the home mission board provided most of the money, we had to abide by their decision.

After a season of prayer and contemplation, I formulated a plan. I would go north at my own expense and ask the Lord to show me a way to make a living. With this in mind, I wrote Brother Hansen and asked if I could serve in Kotzebue on a volunteer basis, and see if the Lord would provide a way for me to support myself and my family.

He replied and said that they had some summer workers there in Kotzebue already, but that I could go to Fort Yukon and take the Missionaries' place while they were on two months furlough.

I wrote to Brother Combs, our mission director and told him I was wanting to resign and pay my own way to Alaska to see if the Lord could sustain me up there. He wrote back and said that he did not believe our work was finished in Hoopa, but he would continue the conventions's part of our salary (the Hoopa church was paying 20% of our support) until I could make a decision. If I decided to stay in Alaska, he would consider that part of my salary as an investment in Alaska missions. And if I came back, I could continue in my present position.

I packed our old second car, a $50.00 1949 Hudson, that was actually in good condition, but looked terrible. I arrived at the Canadian border with an old car and $180.00 cash. The customs inspector was not impressed with the looks of my outfit, and cared even less for my small bank roll. He told me I could not travel the Alaska Highway through Canada to Alaska.

I went back to a camp ground near Mt. Baker, Washington, and camped for 3 days while I prayed and pondered over the situation. I finally decided I would keep going as long as I had some resources. I drove to Seattle, parked the car at a friendly church, and bought a one-way ticket to Fairbanks, Alaska. I arrived in Fairbanks and immediately bought a 1-way ticket to Fort Yukon and paid for a hotel room for the night. I believe I had $1.86 left in my pocket.

I said, "Well, Lord, I don't have any money for food, but I'm going to get there!" The Lord had a surprise left for me, though, for at about 5 p.m. that day, there was a knock on my hotel door. The man standing before me introduced himself as J. T. Burdine, pastor of the University Baptist Church, in Fairbanks.

He told me that Don Rollins, the missionary I was to substitute for, had called him and told him to take me down to the store and buy some groceries. I never did find out how he knew I was in town, or where I was. However, I have learned not to look a gift horse in the mouth, so we took care of the grocery problem.

I spent two months in Fort Yukon. I gave the Lord a June 30th deadline to show me a way to make a living and bring my family to Alaska. I promised Him, that if He did not show me a way I would go back and continue the work in Hoopa.

The deadline came and went with no apparent answer from the Lord, so I wrote my dear wife, Martha, holding the fort in Hoopa, that I would be returning after the Rollins family came home.

Meanwhile, Brother Hansen had sent me a check for $400.00 to help compensate for my stay there. With this money I was able to buy a ticket back to Seattle. But first I decided to fly to Kotzebue and look at this place that was still open for a missionary. I spent two days in Kotzebue and felt very deeply that this was where God wanted us to serve.

I continued on to Anchorage, and visited with the convention personnel for a day before returning to Seattle. They assured me of their desire to have us in the Arctic, but felt they needed to abide by the home mission board's decision. Returning to Hoopa, Martha and I continued to labor in the vineyard. Disappointment did rest on my shoulders that fall, but a wonderful thing happened during this time.

The Lord gave us the privilege of leading a young Caucasian mother of six to a saving faith in Jesus. Carmen was married to a Hoopa Indian. In fact, Carlson, her husband, had been one of my students the first year I taught in Hoopa High School.

She was so wonderfully saved, and her life changed so dramatically that her husband marveled. Martha and I would go to her home on a week-day afternoon and I began to teach her the gospel according to John. Martha would entertain the small children during this time.

Carmen was so open to the word, that she believed God in everything that He said to her through the word, and this accounted for the great change in her life.

In January 1966, I still felt a strong desire to go to Kotzebue. I wrote a five page letter to A. B. Cash, head of Pioneer Missions of our home mission board, and told him that we still felt that God wanted us to go to Kotzebue.

I told him we had prayed all winter that if God did not want us to go to Kotzebue, he would fill the position, and take away our desire to go there. I said He has done neither. Then I went on to explain the life of faith the Lord had led us through the past 12 years, mentioning that our children had been raised out in the woods, and were used to entertaining themselves. They did not have hamburger stands, roller rinks, and movie houses to long for.

I ended by saying that I had tried to go to Alaska as a teacher and a worker but felt that God had led us to be home missionaries for a reason. I thanked him for his kindness and realized they had a real concern and responsibility for the families they sent to faraway places, but I felt that we had been trained for, and could handle this situation. I said I would not write again, but would leave it in his and the Lord's hands.

The next month, February, I received a letter from Brother Cash, thanking me for my good attitude and saying that the missions committee had reconsidered their earlier decision and had decided to appoint us to Kotzebue.

Thus it was that Martha and I and our children landed at the Kotzebue airport June 18, 1966. Two weeks later, Brother Wendell Bellew, a home missions director, visited Kotzebue. A very lovely Christian man, Brother Bellew mentioned during his stay, "Brother Shield, we have your five page letter in our files, and if you ever complain, we'll mail it back to you one page at a time." He smiled when he said it, but I know there was some underlying seriousness to his remarks.

11.

Welcome to Alaska

"Mommy! Mommy! I just flushed the toilet, and water ran all over the floor."

Norman said, "Oh no! I just remembered. The sewage tank is full and plugged up."

It was June 18, 1966 and Martha and I and our family had just debarked from Alaska Airlines' 4-engine Constellation in Kotzebue, Alaska. The children, Ted, Lou Ann, Larry, Danny, and Timmy were there. Bonnie, the eldest, was still in Portland, Oregon attending a musical festival. She would join us within a few days.

All the children were of school age; Bonnie, being a senior in high school and Timmy, the youngest, was in the 2nd grade.

We were met by Norman Harrell, a volunteer church worker. He escorted us to the mission quarters, which proved to be quite spacious and comfortable.

As we were being shown around the building, Larry had to use the bathroom. In a few moments he came running and crying out about the situation in there. We spent the rest of the day looking for a pump and a hose to empty the tank into the sound. (Putting sewage into the sound is no longer practiced.)

The house was heated by an oil-fired furnace, which did not work. Cooking was done on an oil cook stove, which was plugged up with soot. I had never had any experience with oil burning equipment, so the next two weeks my hands were black with oil and soot as I tried to fix these things.

Fortunately since it was the month of June we did not need a lot of heat, so a little electric heater carried us through the next few days. Cleaning the cook stove was not difficult, just messy, so I fixed it right after the septic tank.

Repairing the furnace was another matter. I spent hour after hour taking it apart and putting it together again . Getting the oil to ignite was the problem.

At one time a neighbor phoned and said, "Are you all right over there, Harley? I looked out the window and saw a huge black cloud coming out of your chimney like an explosion."

I said, "I'm ok, just working on the furnace."

One day I visited the little city library and found a small pamphlet on oil furnaces. After studying it, I found how to adjust the ignition points properly, and then it finally worked.

I would have hired someone to do the job, except in those days there were no repair shops. Everyone did his own repairs.

Being new in town, I did not know who to ask, and besides I always tried to be independent. In typical Alaskan bush country fashion, everyone needs to be as self-sufficient as possible. In the Alaskan bush, people either become very competent, or leave the country.

Speaking of being self-sufficient, there are several incidents of Alaskan ingenuity I will mention here:

One time an Eskimo was 50-60 miles out in the country when the plastic tip on the fuel filter of his snow machine broke. He could not think of a way to fix it. He camped there for 3 days, trying to figure it out. Finally he had an inspiration. He had a ball-point pen in his pocket, which he cut with his knife and made a plastic tube. He hooked it up to the fuel line and was able to come home.

Another fellow was stranded in the woods with his snow machine suffering a blown head gasket. After 2 days of fiddling around, he made a gasket out of an old aluminum pie tin, and returned home safely.

Another time a fellow broke the main front spring leaf of his snow machine. He had been caribou hunting and so took some of the sinew from the caribou and some willows and bandaged the spring. He used the willows as splints and wrapped them with sinew. It was winter and about -30 degrees F, so he let it freeze solid and was able to continue his trip.

There is a story about a famous bush pilot, Archie Ferguson, who dented the leading edge of his airplane wing in a landing on a gravel bar. He probably ran into some willows or small trees. To repair it, he laid an old towel around the leading edge and poured water on it. It froze in the right contour and he flew home.

On another occasion, Ferguson broke the tip off one end of his wooden propeller. He was miles from anywhere and wondered what to do. He finally took his sharp hatchet, and trimmed the other tip off. Since they were then fairly well balanced and did not vibrate too much, he was able to fly home. That propeller is now in the Kotzebue museum.

But back to our house. After a lot of trial and error, everything finally worked OK.

By November, I felt everything was going all right at home, so I made a trip to Kobuk by commercial bush plane to hold a week of meetings with the missionaries, Norman and Gunita Harrell. This was the week before the Thanksgiving holiday. My plan was to able to be home before Thanksgiving. On the Saturday I was to come home, a blizzard moved in and stormy weather prevailed for the next week. In those days we had no telephones nor radio communications between the villages and Kotzebue. So Martha just waited, while I spent my first Alaskan Thanksgiving in Kobuk.

While I was there, I had my first taste of Eskimo ice cream. Thanksgiving in the villages is a community affair. At that time everyone gathered in the little church for a sort of pot luck, called Pot Latch by the Eskimos. All the food is put on the tables and everyone sits around the edges of the room and several appointed people serve the rest. One of them asked me if I wanted some Eskimo ice cream, and I said, "Yes," and there was a spoonful put on my plate.

It looked like strawberry ice cream, but when I tried it, it tasted like cod liver oil. Eskimo ice cream is made from the fat of a caribou or moose, but if they do not have that they sometimes use crisco. This is mixed with blueberries, or any other kind of fruit and seasoned liberally with seal oil.

Fresh seal oil is not bad, but rancid seal oil tastes like cod liver oil. After my first taste I looked up and everyone was watching me with bright, twinkling eyes to see what I would do. I knew I would have to finish it, and I did manage to do it by eating a little piece of pilot bread with every bite. However, later I found out that Eskimo ice cream is not bad if made with fresh seal oil.

After the Pot Latch everyone divided the remaining food and took it home. When I was finally able to return to Kotzebue, the Saturday after Thanksgiving, I found Martha and the children living in one bedroom with the electric heater going full blast.

The furnace had ceased to work, and the oil cook stove was plugged up again. Hence came Martha's saying, "Whenever Harley goes somewhere, everything breaks."

12.

The Lord Knows the Way

We had been driving the small boat all night. Half our barrel of gasoline was used up. We hadn't found the channel to head up the Kobuk River to the village of Kobuk. We might as well turn around and return to Kotzebue while we were able.

Since we arrived in Kotzebue in June of 1966, our first summer, we did not get to do much traveling, and we didn't have much money. The old green boat that was left at Kotzebue was designated to go to Kobuk for the volunteer workers up there. They had asked our home mission board for enough money to buy an 18 hp Evinrude outboard engine, and were waiting for an approval.

The plan was for me, Harley Shield, to buy the motor locally at Hanson's Trading Company, and then drive the boat some 300 miles up the Kobuk River to Kobuk.

Kobuk is the last village near the head of the Kobuk River. Of course I was agreeable, for that kind of an outing was exciting. I had a lot of rowing and small boat experience, but had never used an outboard motor before.

It wasn't until the middle of August that I was able to purchase the motor. I asked my 16 year old son, Ted, to accompany me on the trip, which he was more than willing to do.

I had flown to Kiana over the Kobuk delta area once, and over that same area to Selawik once. The Kobuk delta is a maze of channels, sloughs, and dead ends and it is very easy to get lost if you do not know the way. Even though I had flown over twice, I hadn't realized how difficult it would be to stay in the right channel.

I believe this story will show how the Lord takes care of His children. Some would say we were shot with luck, but as a Christian, I don't believe there is such a thing as luck. I would rather call it providential care.

I asked some of the old timers how to find the mouth of the channel and they said, "Well, there's a big marker on it, and once you find that, you kind of work your way up the river."

So Ted and I loaded a lot of food and clothes, camping gear, a barrel of gas, rifles, and cameras. In the middle of August, the sun had started to set, but there was still light all through the night. Therefore the late start, about 4 pm, was not as bad as some might think.

The bad part was that we had never been that route in a boat before, nor were we familiar with the ways of the weather and the lake. We knew the general direction to go, so we headed east from Kotzebue around Pipe Spit and into a freshening easterly wind. This made it a little damp in the boat from the spray that blew across the boat from each wave.

We were headed in the general direction of where we thought one of the three channels were. We finally approached the far side of the lake and the shore was a low lying marshland. The curve of the rivers and abundant growth of reeds and willows hid the mouths of the channels. We would have to position ourselves directly in front of a channel to see it.

We motored along the shore for hours, not really sure of what we were looking for. We never did see the channel marker. It was sort of a twilight condition, which was the reason we kept going. Hour after hour at slow speed, looking for the channel, or ANY channel.

I later realized that it was a good thing we did not find ANY channel, for we would have gone up it and probably gotten hopelessly lost. When you are boating in flat delta land, the banks are about 12' high, and there are no land marks that you can see to guide you.

At any rate, about 6:00 in the morning we had used up half our gas. We had come to the end of Kobuk Lake and I knew that it would open up into Selawik Lake very soon. I had learned that much from studying the maps and overflying the marsh lands. It became apparent that we had missed all the channels of the Kobuk river, and were headed for Selawik, instead of Kobuk. Logic told me that when you use half your gas, and don't know where you are going, it's best to turn around and head for home.

Ted was driving the boat after we turned around, and I was dozing in the early morning hours. After about an hour Ted called out, "That looks like a channel."

By the time I woke up, we could not see the channel. Ted turned the boat around again, and we went back a little ways and sure enough, there was a long straight stretch of water that surely looked like a channel.

I said, "We might as well go up this channel and see where it leads. It looks like a main channel."

After about 2 miles we came to a broad fork in the channel. We could not tell which was up-river because the water was deep and still. We fooled around for about one half hour, dropping things in the river to see which way they floated, and finally determined that the left channel was the upriver channel.

We droned on up the river, winding around back and forth for 2 or 3 hours, when finally we saw a village ahead which turned out to be Noorvik. I knew we were going to be all right then because from Noorvik on there is only one main channel complete with gravel bars and a visible current.

Another 3 hours and we arrived at Kiana. We have a Baptist mission there, which at that time was staffed by Valeria Sherrard, our single-lady missionary.

We walked up to the mission just in time for supper. Valeria was surprised to see us and welcomed us. After warming up, eating and visiting for a couple of hours, we bought enough gas to refill our barrel, and decided to continue upriver a few more miles and make camp for the night.

The rest of the trip was very long, but very beautiful. The Kobuk River is a clear blue, and flows through pristine Arctic wilderness. I couldn't stop taking pictures, and when evening came the third day, the sun set in the western sky with a blood red beauty, equaling any that I had ever seen!

We camped out one more night at about 20 miles below Ambler. The next day we continued on past Ambler and Shung-nak all the way to Kobuk, about a 9 hour trip.

We pulled up to the beach in the little village of Kobuk and were welcomed by Norman and Gunita Harrell, the volunteer missionaries for that village. They were glad to see us, mainly because they had been waiting for the boat and motor all summer.

The bush mail plane had just landed at the same time, with one available seat. I elected to go back to Kotzebue right away, and left Ted to return the following day with all of our camping gear.

The return trip home was quicker, but not nearly as interesting. I am reminded of the little chorus we sing,

"The Lord knows the way through the wilderness, all I have to do is follow."

There's no doubt in my mind that God prevented us from taking the wrong channel, and surely pointed us to the right channel.

13.

Traveling

I was really glad I had used wood screws instead of boat nails when I made our small outboard runabout. The beating it was taking crossing the Selawik Lake would stress any boat.

When a newcomer comes to the bush and wants to travel, he has to have an 'outfit'. In summer he needs a boat, motor and all sorts of camping equipment. Even then, he needs warm as well as cool weather clothing, plus hip boots and rain gear. When you travel you are completely on your own, and have to have everything that you could need in any possible situation.

To get our outfit, the first task was to build a boat. So in the summer of 1967 we bought a Lugar 20' plywood boat kit. When we were finished, we installed an Evinrude 33 hp outboard motor on the transom.

Martha and I then decided to take a trip to Selawik, about 100 miles away by water. The trip over was uneventful, and took about 6 hours.

Two days later, when it was time to go home, there was a stiff 20-knot headwind blowing across the lake from the West. Being from California and used to jumping in the car and going in any kind of weather, I figured we could make it, even though all the villagers cautioned us to wait until the wind died down.

We spent 8 hours plunging through the waves, rocking up and down, and getting soaked and we were still only half way home. We finally pulled ashore in the narrows at the end of the lake and built a fire to dry out and warm up.

It was while crossing the lake and being slapped around by the waves that I was glad that I had used wood screws instead of boat nails to put the boat together. Sometimes the boat would shudder when hit by a wave, and boat nails could have worked loose.

After about three hours the wind died down a little and we spent the next five hours going through the narrows and traversing another lake.

It was just getting dark when we rounded the last point and saw the lights of Kotzebue twinkling in the distance. The old hymn "The Lights of Home" took on a new meaning for us.

Then I also knew why Eskimos could lay around for 2 or 3 days waiting for the wind to die down. Usually, about 2 or 3 in the morning we would hear outboards starting up. The people would know when to travel and when not to. Strangely enough, they usually got to their destinations about the same time as the pilgrims who were struggling against the weather.

From this I learned why the natives won't give advice to new white people. They know there will only be an argument, and the white folks will go their own ways anyhow. I also learned the meaning of the saying, "When in Rome, do as the Romans do."

14.

Putting on a Show

"If this crazy old motor wouldn't die every time I turned my back, I could get the anchor out at the right place," I muttered to myself, after several tries at anchoring off the beach in a stiff onshore wind.

Learning continues daily for the newcomer to the Arctic. My experiences in boating often provided a great show for onlookers.

Our first boat was an old green tub left by the former missionary. It was about 20' long and about as sea worthy as a log. The engine left by the former missionary was a worn out 35 hp Evinrude.

This was one of the OLD Evinrudes that weighed about 180 lbs. I had never touched an outboard motor before coming to Alaska, but I set out to learn all I could. After hours of studying and working and fiddling, I finally got it running

I mounted it on this old green boat and started using it. Sometimes it would just stop, and I could not get it started again for a long time. Another chronic problem with it was that it would not idle. As soon as it got below a certain rpm, it would die.

We used to anchor our boat in front of the village. I watched the Eskimos, and they would come up close to the beach, turn the motor off, and throw the anchor out at just the right time, about 30 feet out from the beach.

Then the boat would have enough headway, so that it would continue on and gently land on the beach. After the boat was unloaded and everybody was out, they would tie the stern line to an anchoring point on the beach, then pull the boat out into the water by the anchor line to a safe distance from the beach. They were still close enough to the beach to allow the person to jump off the stern in his hip boots and walk up to the shore. Then they would tighten the stern line to the position they wanted and the boat was made fast.

This process is rather easy when the wind is calm or blowing from off the shore. However, when we have a west wind, with small waves blowing right on the shore, we don't have enough time to correct any mistakes.

This was the condition of the waves and wind one day when I tried to anchor my boat the Eskimo way. A nice stiff west wind was blowing right on the beach. I came in a little too fast, because the engine wanted to die. At what I thought was just the right time, I scrambled up into the bow and threw out the anchor. The engine died, and the boat began to swing around to the beach and I realized I was too close. I frantically began to restart the engine, and got it going just before the stern ground into the gravel. I gave it enough power to get the boat over the anchor and then I ran forward and pulled up the anchor.

The boat was pitching up and down and rolling about. I got the anchor aboard, motored out a little bit and turned it around and tried again. This time when the boat swung around I was too far out. Every time I left the motor to throw out the anchor, the motor would die. I went through this process about 6 times before I finally got it right.

After I'd tied the stern line and jumped on the beach, I looked up and the whole bank above the beach was lined with interested spectators, many of them smiling and watching the "nalagmi" (white man).

It was a rather humbling experience.

15.

Running Aground in the Boat

*The crashing noise and the sliding halt of our boat
on the gravel beach brought our attention back from
the broken jar of chipped beef to the business of
watching where we were going, a little too late.*

One of my favorite sayings concerning boating in the Kotzebue area is that, "I know where all the sandbars are. I have hit
them all more than once!" However, running aground in our new
little plywood runabout in this story was just plain foolishness.

This was the summer of 1968, our second season of boating.
Martha, our youngest son, Timothy, and I decided to ride up the
Noatak River on a beautiful Saturday. We were speeding along
about 35 miles an hour with two outboard engines humming
along beautifully. When we were about 40 miles up river, we
decided to have a little snack while traveling. We asked Timmy
to get a small jar of chipped beef and some sandwich materials
from the back of the boat.

He was having trouble opening the sealed lid on the chipped beef, so I told him to get a pair of pliers and try to work it off. Martha was watching him as he struggled there between us, and I was watching the river. The lid popped off, and Timmy cried out, "I got it off, but there's a little glass that broke off into the meat!"

This diverted my attention from watching the river, and Martha and I both became engrossed in watching Timmy try to get the glass out. I completely forgot about driving the boat.

Suddenly, the boat gave a crash and a lurch and bounced to a standstill. The two outboard motors were roaring at almost full throttle, the lower unit rising and falling into the sand and gravel, the propellers throwing mud and gravel into the boat and everywhere else!

I shut the motors off, and we sat there in stunned silence, not yet fully realizing what had happened. We climbed out of the boat and looked around. The water's edge was about 25' away. We were fortunate we had run up on a shelving beach, rather than into a cut bank which runs straight up and down from the water's edge.

Needless to say, the pilot, me, felt rather foolish, but very thankful that we were unhurt.

We examined the motors and found they were relatively undamaged. We took the floorboards out of the boat and found that except for a bruise or two on the hull, it was still seaworthy. Now we had to figure a way to get it back into the water.

Finally, by removing both motors, the portable gas tanks and all the other heavy things, we were able to work the boat down to the water's edge.

After refloating the boat, we reinstalled the motors, loaded everything, and were ready to go, a little wiser from the experience. We were a little bit crestfallen, and decided to return to Kotzebue. The trip home was enjoyable, and our attitudes much more watchful. We weren't anxious to repeat the experience.

16.

Frozen Peanut Butter Sandwiches

My peanut butter and jam sandwiches were frozen solid. Charlie was contentedly munching his dried fish, pilot bread and seal oil. Where had this old California boy gone wrong, I thought.

Newcomers to the Arctic have to learn a lot of things the hard way. I mentioned in one of the other stories that the native people do not like to give advice because newcomers just argue about it and don't accept it. However, the natives keep a watchful eye over newcomers, especially when they travel in the bush, and I am sure they get plenty of laughs.

The winter of 1968 was in full swing and I had just purchased my first snow machine, a used 1965 model. An Eskimo friend asked me if I would take him to the North end of what we call Kobuk Lake. He had his nets set under the ice at a spot about 20 miles from Kotzebue. The Eskimos are able to fish under the ice all winter because they have devised a way to put their nets under the early winter ice in such a way that they can be pulled out and checked for fish at regular intervals.

The local people go out to a selected fishing spot when the ice is only about a foot thick, and chop two holes in the ice about 100' apart. They drop a rope through one hole and somehow are able to fish the end up through the other hole. Then they attach their fish net to it and pull it down through the hole so that it is stretched out under the ice between the holes. They have weights on the nets to hold them down low enough so that the tops of the nets will not freeze to the new ice that is forming on the under side of the pack ice. The lake ice will get five or six feet thick during the course of the winter.

In order to check the nets, all they have to do is break free the holes, and pull the net up and remove the fish.

This is what Charlie Kiana wanted to do when he asked me to take him out to his fishing spot. The weather was rather cold, especially for me, at about 20 degrees below zero, but it was a beautiful day, otherwise.

I prepared the snow machine and sled, got some extra clothes and made a lunch to carry with me. Then I went to Charlie's place and picked him up, along with his equipment, and we made the long journey out to the fishing spot.

After we arrived I began to help Charlie free up his net. I soon learned this was a lot more work than I thought. Of course, his spot was marked with poles, so we could find where to dig. First we had to shovel away snow that had drifted into the holes, then we had to chip away the 2' of ice that formed since his last visit. We had to make the hole big enough for the net and fish to be pulled through. These fish are called Shee fish and can be as large as 40 pounds, but average about 12 to 15 pounds. Therefore, the hole needs to be fairly large.

It didn't take long for my back to start complaining, and I marvel at the industry and tenacity of these Eskimo men. But we kept at it and after about an hour of hard work, were able to pull the net and gather some fish.

When the net was pulled back into the water before it froze, and the open holes were carefully covered with pieces of cardboard, to keep ice from freezing too thick before the next time, Charlie said it was time for lunch.

I brought out my camp stove and started melting ice for coffee or tea, whichever we preferred. Charlie brought out his lunch of dried fish, dried caribou, some seal oil and some pilot bread crackers, and began eating. I opened my lunch of peanut butter sandwiches, that I had carefully prepared. They were frozen solid! I was learning quickly why pilot bread and dried meats were preferred in the winter.

The best I could do was to prop my sandwiches up in the back of the camp stove and try to thaw them out. Needless to say, I did not enjoy my lunch very much and I learned a thing or two about "traveling food" in the winter.

The Eskimo carries food that won't freeze up, such as dried meats, fish and crackers, and a little seal oil on the side. Seal oil is a great source of energy and pretty necessary when you are traveling in extreme cold, for your body is putting out a lot of heat and that uses a great amount of energy.

Charlie was pleased with the 30 or 40 fish he got out of the net that day, and we were able to return home without any problems. I enjoyed the outing, even though my lunch was a complete flop.

17.

James Hensley, Itinerant Preacher

*I would have felt more comfortable if I had known
what James was preaching about. He preached in his
native Inupiat language and the Eskimos loved it.
However, I did not understand the language, and
could only pray that he was preaching the gospel as
recorded in God's word, the Bible.*

James Oomivik Hensley had come to us one day as we were
preparing to go to a Bible conference in Selawik. He asked if he
could travel with us. Little in stature, he did not present a
domineering appearance, but he was experienced in the ways of
Arctic travel.

We did not know James very well. We knew that he had been
attending the Kotzebue Church of God for some time, but we
were agreeable to his fellowship.

As with many Eskimos at that time, James did not have a
regular job. He lived a more subsistence kind of life with occa-

sional seasonal types of jobs. This meant he had time to travel more than the average person.

After the Bible conference, he indicated a desire to travel with me on my snow machine gospel trips. At that time I was making a week and a half tour of all four missions about once a month in the winter. I would go to a village and stay one or two nights and have preaching each night, and then travel to the next village. The round trip would be about 500-600 miles.

So it evolved that James became a traveling companion. In the beginning, James would share short testimonies in his native language during the meetings. Later on he became more adept at preaching, so I encouraged him to share each time.

Our program eventually went something like this: first we would sing hymns from the Baptist hymnal; then I would share from God's word for 20 minutes or so. Then we would have testimonies and prayer time. Next we would sing songs in the Eskimo language - which they dearly loved to do. Last of all James would close the evening by preaching in the native tongue, which they also dearly loved to hear.

At first I was apprehensive about his preaching, because I could not understand what he was saying. As time went by I found that he was not very deep doctrinally, and most of his preaching was more of a testimony type.

We traveled together for many years and had a good number of adventures together, and the Eskimos heard him gladly.

After 2 years James talked to me and said he wanted to be a Baptist and would like to be baptized. I told him he needed to come before the church, give his testimony and ask to be baptized.

When he came forward during the invitation one evening, I asked him to tell the church why he had come forward. He turned and said in his humble way, "I want to be one of you fellas!"

I asked, "Do you want to be baptized?"

He said, "Yes."

After about 10 years of serving the Lord in this fashion, James contracted cancer and within a year went to be with the Lord.

His big family Bible, with all his favorite Bible passages underlined, is now resting on the pulpit table at the church in Selawik - The Selawik Baptist Mission - as a gift from James. He never went to school, but did learn to read the Bible. When he knew he was going to die, he asked his sister-in-law to see that his Bible went to the Selawik church.

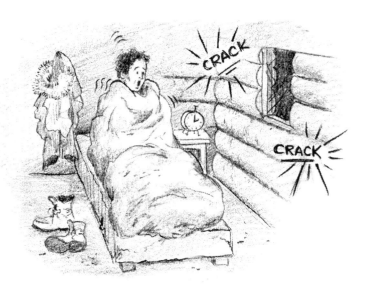

18.

Sled Stories —
New Year's Eve

The next trail marker was not to be found, no matter how hard I tried. The pitch black night would not allow the snow machine's head light to pick out anything resembling a marker in the fresh trackless snow.

Before we got into airplane flying, we did a lot more traveling to the villages by snow machine and sled. One year I decided to go to Selawik for New Year's Eve, which happened to be on a Saturday night. The days are very short in December so by the time I started, it was late afternoon and getting very dark.

The snow machine trails in our area go from village to village. They are marked by tripods made from spruce saplings about 300 feet apart on the trail. These are renewed periodically by the men who receive money from the Alaska Road Commission, or from Highway funds.

Of course, between renewal periods some of these tripods fall down because of wind and weather. The tripods are necessary to keep travelers from getting lost during blizzards, snow storms, fog or dark nights.

When some of the tripods are missing, especially on a curve in the trail, it is very hard to find the next one at night. This can be doubly difficult if a person is traveling after a fresh snow fall and no tracks are visible. This was the case when I was traveling New Year's Eve.

About half-way to Selawik from Noorvik, I stopped at the Singauruk shelter cabin for a snack and a cup of coffee. The village people have shelter cabins at strategic places along the trail for folks who are storm bound, or otherwise in trouble. There is usually a stove, plywood bunk, a saw or an axe, and a few pieces of firewood to get a fire started. This can be a welcome sight when needed.

I started from the shelter cabin and out into the flat tundra to travel the 30 miles to Selawik. There were no tracks to follow because of the fresh snow, so I had to rely on the tripods that came into view one at a time as my headlights revealed them.

All went well for a few miles, but suddenly, I came to a place where I could not find the next tripod. Since it was so dark, and the very clear dust-free air did not allow the headlight beam to shine very far, I drove back and forth and circled but could not find the next tripod. I began to have so many tracks that I was afraid that I might not be able to find the trail back to the shelter cabin. So I elected to return there before I was helplessly lost.

I believe that one of the secrets of successful travel in the bush is to always have an optional course of action, a back door, so to speak. Once you use up all your options, you are committed to your original course, which sometimes can be fatal.

Thus I retraced my trail back to the shelter cabin, resigning myself to spending New Year's Eve in solitude.

Well, it wasn't so bad. I had my trail food, coffee, a good candle, and all my necessary camping gear. I got a fire going in the rusty old stove and spent a quiet night, at least most of the night.

About 2 o'clock in the morning I was awakened by a tremendous loud cracking sound. I listened fearfully for a few moments, but there was dead silence. Then I realized that 'cabins talk' (as Eskimos say) in cold weather. In other words, the contraction of logs in cold weather causes the loud sound.

In the winter the sun comes up around 9 or 10 o'clock, so by the time I was ready to leave, it was beginning to be light. I was curious to see what had happened to the tripods the night before. I soon came to the place where all my tracks were circling and turning and noticed that I had passed within 10 feet of one marker, but it was so dark I had not seen it.

Then I discovered the real problem of the night before. The trail made a curve to the right and the next three tripods had fallen and were covered with snow. I had been trying to find the tripod straight ahead, and of course would never have found it. I'm glad I returned to the cabin.

The difference between safe travel and dangerous, sometimes fatal travel is told right here in this story. Inexperienced people have not always learned patience and tend to keep traveling when lost in the dark or in a blizzard, until they run out of gas, sometimes 40 or 50 miles from where they should have been.

Sometimes they are fortunate and strong enough to walk in, or be rescued, but many times they pay for their mistake with their lives. The wise thing to do is to pull a tarp over yourself and stay where you are until the weather clears, even if it takes a day or two.

With the coming of daylight and with fresh snow covering the trail and good visibility, I made a fast uneventful trip to Selawik. I arrived there in time to light the oil stoves and gather the people together for Sunday School and church services. Amen!

19.

Learning To Fly

"When you pass the pilot's written test, let me know and I'll pay your way down here and pay for your flying lessons."

Thus the open door I had prayed for appeared before my eyes, so to speak.

About 1968 I decided it would be useful to be able to fly, because we ministered to five missions, with a potential of 13, in an area of a 250 mile radius from the center of Kotzebue.

But the problem was that the Alaska Baptist Convention that employed us was pretty negative about their home missionaries flying, because of bad experiences in the past.

In fact, one of the reasons they approved of letting us go to Kotzebue was because I did NOT fly!

However, Martha and I decided we wanted to let the Lord decide what we should do. I would pray and ask the Lord, "Well, if you want me to fly, you'll have to open a way to let me fly."

So, in 1970, the Alaska Baptists invited people to a Layman's Crusade. One of the men who attended was Jack Maxwell from Tyler, Texas. He came to preach in the First Baptist Church in Eagle River, Alaska. I was invited to preach with him.

Jack Maxwell had a logging and sawmill operation in Texas. He owned his own airplane and was an accomplished pilot. He became interested in our work in the Arctic and encouraged me to become a pilot. Then he went home.

That fall, our high school offered a pilot's ground school instruction course, as part of their adult education program. Our oldest son, Ted, and I decided to enroll. There were about 21 in the class; middle aged folks, teachers, and some kids.

About half way through the class, another teacher who was a pilot and owned a Cessna 172, offered to take the Wycliffe Bible Translator back to his home in Noorvik. He also invited the student body president and another friend to go with them.

The whole village of Kotzebue was stunned that Sunday afternoon to learn that the plane had climbed to about 100 feet on take off, stalled, and spun down to crash and burn on the runway. They were all killed.

The next time our ground school class convened, there were only eight present. The others never came back. But Ted and I decided to continue.

A couple of days later, Brother Maxwell called me at 3 am (from Texas where it was 8 am) and I told him I was taking ground school.

He said, "When you pass the written test, let me know and I'll pay your way down here and I'll pay for your flying lessons."

I considered that an 'open door', the direction of the Lord that I was looking for.

In Texas I stayed at the Maxwell home and Jack loaned me a car to drive to the Cherokee County Airport in Jacksonville, about 13 miles away. After I soloed, he hired an instructor to fly with me about 6 hours a day to groom me for the check-out ride.

With his help, I was able to pass the check-out test and received certification in just 30 days, on March 30, 1971.

I went home with a license to fly, but I didn't know where I'd get a plane. We started praying for an airplane.

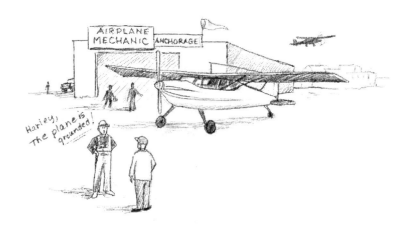

20.

We Get an Airplane

The scene is the Kiana airstrip. An anxious traveler is trying to convince air taxi operator Lee Stahle into flying him to Kotzebue. It was about 40 degrees below zero. Lee kept refusing, maintaining that it was too cold. At that point a green Cessna 170 landed on the frozen river and parked. "What about that plane. He's flying."

"Oh, that's that crazy Harley," Lee responded.

I had come home to Kotzebue with a pilot's license and no airplane. While Martha and I were praying about the Lord's will concerning it, one of our church members, who had a small Piper Pacer (PA - 22), offered to let me use it to practice flying.

At that time Martha was not interested in flying, but sometimes she would go to the airport and watch me do touch-and-gos. As she was watching, the thought came to her, "Why am I standing down here? I could be up there, too!"

The Lord gave Martha the confidence to fly with me, knowing that "underneath are the everlasting arms."

We continued to pray and search for an acceptable airplane. we finally found a 1947 ragwing Cessna (metal body with fabric covered wings) for $5,000.00. With a loan at the bank and a deferred down payment, we bought it. Because the Cessna 170 rag wing was notorious for stall-spin crashes, two men in our church were actually praying that I would not buy the airplane. Other than that it was a great and forgiving airplane. So Martha and I began our adventures in the air.

As a novice Arctic bush pilot, I did not know that experienced pilots generally do not like to fly in temperatures below -30 degrees Fahrenheit. Consequently, the first two winters, we were flying when it was 50 to 60 degrees below zero. If I could get it started, I flew it.

This probably explains why when I took the plane to Anchorage for its first annual checkup the next summer, the compression in one of the six cylinders was zero, one was 10 and one was 30. Since the minimum should be 70 pounds, the mechanic said, "This plane is grounded."

A phone call to the bank gave an "OK" to refinance our loan for $3000.00 more for a reconditioned engine.

With our 'new' engine, we continued to fly through the next winter, making the same mistakes.

21.

Running Out of Gas

The airplane lifted off easily, and at about fifty feet altitude, the engine quit. I immediately switched tanks and worked the primer. I almost had the engine started, when we touched down again on the ice.

Generally speaking, planes run out of gas due to pilot error, which could be fuel mismanagement, or pure carelessness. My one and only time of running out of gas occurred during my early flying years in our 1947 Cessna 170 rag wing. (Metal covered body, fabric covered wings.)

James Hensley, my Eskimo preaching partner, and I were flying back from a Kobuk gospel trip and had landed on the ice at Selawik for the night. We were still using wheels, for it was early during the fall freeze-up, and we did not have any snow drifts as yet.

This airplane had two small gas tanks in the wings, holding 17 gallons each, which was a small amount for Alaska flying.

Along with the small supply were the old-time gas gauges in the wing-roots with the dials inside the cabin. These promptly froze up during the cold winter months and were totally useless. Of course pilots do not rely on gauges, but use the hours flown to monitor fuel.

At the time we landed in Selawik, I still had fuel in the tank I was using and I planned to use the other tank later on the way to Kotzebue. Naturally, pilots who happen to read this will immediately recognize I failed to switch to the full tank when landing. Seems the big problem with flying, is staying alive while learning the game correctly.

The next morning we got the plane running, preparatory to going on to Kotzebue. During the preflight, because it was so difficult to climb up to the top of the wing, I did not visually check the fuel supply, but rather relied on elapsed time of the day before.

To expose the flaw in my thinking was the fact that unbeknownst to me, someone had drained gasoline from the wing tanks to use in a snow machine engine. The 80/87 aviation fuel runs fine in snow machines and outboard engines.

Fortunately frozen rivers offer long runways. We taxied out to the middle of the river and began the take-off roll. It was then that trouble began. As soon as we were airborne we were out of gas!

I didn't really realize at the time that the gasoline had been stolen. I figured that I had just miscalculated my flying time as the reason we ran out. Consequently, my second error of the day was that I did not visually check the other tank.

From these experiences one learns not to assume anything.

We fired up the old plane and took off again, flying the 90 miles or so back to Kotzebue. The trip takes one over a lot of tundra and then Kobuk Lake and across the fifteen-mile wide peninsula to Kotzebue. This section is filled with small lakes, rolling hills, and lots of willows.

Just after we crossed the peninsula and as we reached the frozen Kotzebue sound the engine quit again. I immediately radioed Kotzebue that the engine was out and I was making an emergency landing on the ice at the edge of town.

Usually the ice in this section freezes up in broken jagged pieces, but this year it was smooth. I was able to make a successful landing. I finally visually inspected the other gas tank. You guessed it, it was dry!

It was then I realized that someone must have stolen the gas the night before. I was glad there was enough left to get across the peninsula, otherwise the plane would have come down in the willows or on the tundra, and been destroyed. We could have been seriously hurt or killed.

I radioed the flight service that we were OK, then we walked to my house about 2 miles away. We took my snow machine and sled, went to my barrels of gas at the airport, and got 10 gallons of gas to take to the airplane.

After gassing up the plane, I flew to the airport, tied down the wings and went home. I praised the Lord for His protection, and have never flown again without visually inspecting the gas supply before taking off.

22.

Bending My First Propeller

*The tail rose straight up in the air. The propeller
ground a hole in the runway gravel slowing the full
throttle engine to a halt. The tail fell back to earth
along with my heart. My new $3000.00 engine? What
have I done?*

Our little Cessna 170 had a new remanufactured engine with
about 50 hours flying time on it. It was the fall season and the
winds were rather gusty. Of course, it doesn't have to be any
special time for the winds to be gusty in the Northwest Arctic.
But this day in particular, they certainly were.

I had just made what I thought was a successful landing with
a 30 knot crosswind, and was attempting to taxi to my tie down
spot.

Taxiing with a stiff crosswind is difficult in a plane with
conventional landing gear (tail dragger), because the wind blowing on the tail makes the plane want to be like a weather vane

and turn into the wind. Therefore, with the wind on the right side, one has to use the left brake rather severely. This in turn heats up the brake lining until it loses its effectiveness. Then you have to stop and let the brakes cool before continuing on.

I had worked my way along the length of the runway and was almost to the point where I could finish my taxiing heading directly into the wind. The left brake became hot and I swung into the wind and stopped to let the brake cool off. Dallas Cross, one of the young men in Kotzebue, was working with four others loading fish on a DC 6 transport plane. He came over and asked if I needed help. He said, "We can push the plane over to your tie down spot for you."

"No thanks," I replied, "I'm almost there. I can make it."

Dallas said, "OK." and walked back to his work.

Now when I had stopped and swung into the wind a little ridge of soft dirt and gravel had built up in front of the right tire. In order to overcome that I pushed the throttle to the fire wall to get a short blast of power. To my dismay, the tail rose straight up in the air. I made a stab for the throttle and missed. Before I could do anything else, the propeller dug a hole about one foot deep in the gravel, and the engine ground to a halt.

The tail, of course, fell back to the earth and I sat there in silence, looking at my ruined propeller through the windshield. Dallas walked over with a disgusted look on his face and asked if I wanted him and his fellow workers to push the plane over to the tie down spot.

It was a crestfallen pilot who said, "Yes, thank you very much."

The five young men pushed and man-handled the plane, while I sat very quietly in the cockpit and reflected on my foolishness. Later I had a mechanic examine the engine and propeller, and it was determined that no damage had been done internally, and it did not require a major overhaul. With a new propeller installed, I was free to fly again and learn some more the hard way.

1947 Rag-Wing
Cessna
170

23.

Our Last Flight in 93 Victor

"Kotzebue Radio, this is Cessna 93 Victor."

"Cessna 93 Victor, this is Kotzebue Radio. Go ahead."

"This is 93 Victor. Our engine is running very rough. We are about four miles east, and are making a precautionary landing on skis."

"Roger, 93 Victor. Do you need any help?"

"93 Victor. No, thanks."

About January the year following the great bent propeller incident, Martha and I flew out of Shungnak, Alaska, at 64 degrees below zero. The plane took an extraordinarily long time to become air borne. Being on skiis, and on the river ice, we went around two bends in the river before the plane would lift off. Then, during the next month the plane seemed to have less power, but being a novice, I did not realize what was wrong.

In February our oldest son, Ted, was getting married in Tuntatuliak, a small village near Bethel. This is about 250 miles West of Anchorage on the Kuskokwim River. So one cold February morning, Martha, Tim, (our youngest son), and I took off with the plane fully loaded for Tunt.

As we circled around Kotzebue, the engine began to sound rough. Thinking the spark plugs were a little fouled, I leaned the fuel mixture, hoping to clean the carbon off the plugs. The engine immediately began to miss and run on only three of its six cylinders. The engine rpm dropped to about 1850. We were barely staying in the air.

From the back of my mind came a phrase I had read. "In case of engine trouble, it is better to land while you still have a little power, than to wait until the engine completely quits."

Since it was winter and we were on skiis, it was easy to find a place to land. I radioed Kotzebue flight service and told them of our trouble and that we were landing. After we had landed, I informed them that we were safely down. They asked if we needed help, and I said, "No, we will be OK."

Still thinking it was the spark plugs, Tim and I removed them and found they were in good condition. Replacing the spark plugs and starting the engine, I found it would not produce enough power to even taxi. There was nothing left to do but start walking what I thought was only four miles to Kotzebue. (We later found that we were really eight miles from Kotzebue.)

As we walked, we found the snow deeper and more difficult to walk in than I had anticipated. About the time we were getting a little discouraged, we heard a snow machine coming through some willows toward us. I said "That sounds like our son Danny's snow machine; but it can't be. He's working at his job in Kotzebue."

But as the machine approached, we discovered that it was indeed Danny. "Danny, what are you doing here? We thought you were working!"

"No, I just got a new shot gun and I took the day off to try it out."

Danny stayed at the plane and hunted while Tim and I borrowed his snow machine and sled. Martha rode in the sled behind and we went back to Kotzebue. There we left Martha at home. I got my snow machine and sled and Tim drove Danny's and we two took Danny's sled back to him. Tim and I unloaded the luggage and gear from the plane into my sled and we returned to Kotzebue.

Because of the sudden winds we often get in the Arctic, it was necessary to tie the plane down securely. So I filled four 53 gallon drums with stove oil and took two trips and spent the rest of the afternoon hauling it out to the plane for tie-downs. There the plane would sit until could figure a way to get it back to town.

24.

How the Lord Got Into
My Airplane Business Instead of Me

*"Lord! This ragged old Cessna is the best I can do,
and it's not good enough! If you want me to fly you
will have to do the providing. If not, I won't fly
anymore."*

The Cessna 170 was 8 miles outside of Kotzebue, on skis,
and tied down to four drums of oil, and had an engine that would
barely turn. My two sons, Danny and Larry, and I came up with
a plan to get it back to Kotzebue. We would round up five or six
snow machines and tie two of them to each landing gear and one
to the tail to kind of steer it with.

We tried it, and everything went according to plan, but we
could not control the steering. The plane ended up in four feet of
really soft snow, about one half mile from where we started.

All the crew went back to the oil drums and brought them to
the plane for tie downs.

About a week later, Danny and I tried Plan Two. This plan was to remove the skis, turn them around, and tow the plane backwards. My snow machine had broken down, so I used Martha's. It was about 25 degrees below zero. We worked all afternoon lifting one side of the plane at a time in the soft snow, and turning the skis around.

There were only the two of us, but by about 4 pm we were ready to try it. When I started Martha's snow machine it would not run normally, but only as I used the primer. That meant the carburetor had frozen. We retied the plane and I coaxed the snow machine back to Kotzebue using the primer all the way.

I was pretty discouraged. The airplane was broken, my snow machine was broken, Martha's snow machine was broken. Well, I said, "At least our pickup is still running."

I arrived home about 5:30 and was in the house warming up and nursing a grouch, when the phone rang. It was about five minutes after six. Martha had just gotten off work and was phoning to tell me that the pickup wouldn't start.

I said, "OK, I'll walk down and see if I can get it started."

On the way, I was cold, tired, hungry and disgusted. With a very poor attitude I said to the Lord, "This is the best I can do, buying this ragged old Cessna 170. I don't have any business trying to buy an airplane with my limited income. If YOU WANT ME TO FLY, you're going to have to provide the plane, because I'm not taking out any more loans."

I was able to get the truck started and we came home, ate dinner, and went to bed.

The next morning after Martha went to work, I had my prayer time and apologized to the Lord for my bad attitude. Also, that day I read an article about faith and trust in the Lord that helped me to turn it all over to the Lord and just rest in Him. I began to realize the reason we don't turn things completely over to the Lord is because we're afraid He'll say, "NO", and we can't have our own way.

At this point, then, it was completely up to the Lord whether I flew the airplane or not.

The following week I gathered up sons Danny and Larry, and three of their friends and their snow machines, and we went out to pull the plane in to the airport. Now plan two worked beautifully, along with much scary teetering and sliding down hills. We managed to get the plane safely to the airport.

A day or two later I asked the airplane mechanic to look at the engine to see if he could determine what was wrong. He removed the oil screen, reached his hand into the crankcase, and pulled out a collapsed oil filter and handfuls of aluminum shavings.

Apparently what had happened way back in January, when we flew out of Shungnak, at 64 degrees below zero, the crankcase oil had not been completely warmed up. This caused a frozen lump of oil to clog up the oil screen and collapse it. This, then allowed the oil to begin flowing again, but not before the left three cylinders were badly scored, shaving off aluminum into the oil system and crankcase. The engine was totally ruined.

About a week from this time, Pastor Virgil Chron of the Melodeon Road Baptist Church in Anchorage called me and said the Lord had laid it on his heart to get me another airplane.

His church took out a loan of $14,000.00 and bought a 1953 Cessna 180, and presented the keys to me about two weeks after the phone call.

Now! This was the Lord's airplane! Any time it needed fixing and money for parts, I would tell Him, "Lord, your plane needs fixing!"

Also, at this time, the Lord raised up a third man to help with this airplane ministry. We already had Jack Maxwell, and Pastor Virgil Chron. The third man's name was Coy Cole. He was a Baptist airplane mechanic who had just opened a business of repairing and rebuilding airplanes in Anchorage. He undertook the maintenance of this more sophisticated plane. If I had the money, I paid the bill. If I didn't or only part of it Coy took care of it.

This was how God gained control and released me of the burden. He has been providing the airplanes and the financial means, by one way or another ever since.

Where God guides, He provides!

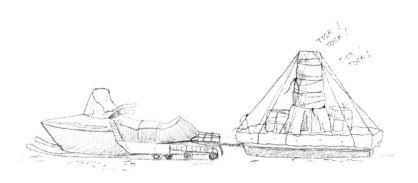

25.

Moving 100 Miles by Snow Machine

If you have ever tried to move a refrigerator, couch and freezer one hundred miles by snowmobile, you know how much trouble we had. But our budget was limited and we needed these things. Yes, even above the Arctic Circle one needs refrigeration and a freezer,

In 1978, Martha and I resigned the church in Kotzebue in order to devote our time preaching and visiting in the five missions. These were Selawik, Kiana, Ambler, Shungnak, and Kobuk. We tried to get another pastor for Kotzebue.

So in the spring of 1978 we moved to Selawik. The housing there was a small two bedroom apartment attached to the one room church house. We were able to move the small things, boxes etc., in the Cessna 180 airplane that we had. But the large things like the refrigerator, freezer, couch, etc., called for another type of transportation.

Being on a limited budget, as usual, I decided to transport them by snow machine and flat-bed sled. The distance from Kotzebue to Selawik is a little over 100 miles by land. It takes about five or six hours one way, and about 15 gallons of gasoline round trip, so it's pretty economical, and a lot cheaper than shipping by air freight.

Transporting the refrigerator and freezer called for some ingenuity, as the trail could be quite rough at times. I found an old inner spring mattress at the dump, and used it for padding.

The appliances seemed to fare quite well, and we got them all there. My crowning achievement was transporting Martha's grandfather clock safely by this method. I took about four more trips and numerous plane flights for a finish.

26.

Baptism in the Arctic

*"Emma, I promise you the baptismal water won't be
ice cold. I'll heat it on the primus stove," but Emma
was hard to convince.*

The time of rejoicing had come to the Arctic. After nearly 16
years of ministering to the Eskimos in Selawik, we were finally
to have a baptismal service. We had six candidates and this was
to be quite an affair, and actually took three days to complete.

We nearly had a baptism in the first year we came here when
a seventeen-year-old girl had been a candidate, but the church
decided she was not ready.

Now this was in April and baptism by immersion in the
Arctic winter is not an easy thing to accomplish. The water is
pretty hard in April, in fact you can walk on it, for it is frozen to
about five feet thick.

In the winter, the villagers chip ice and fill the water barrels
in their homes. They also dip water from holes in the river ice,

kept open by using what the Eskimos call a "tauk" (pronounced "toke"). It is made by lashing a chisel or sharpened crowbar to the end of a long pole. Then by an up and down motion they chip a hole in the ice. I can assure you that making a hole through about five feet of ice is a lot of hard work!

These holes are kept open all winter by constant use and by covering them with a piece of cardboard or plywood. The children and women are the water haulers, commonly called "woman's work" in the villages. "Man's work" is to get the wood and to do the hunting.

For our baptismal service we had to have a water source, the river, then a suitable tub or tank had to be found. Also, the people involved at this time were in four different villages, covering a distance of over 250 air miles, and natives travel in winter mostly by snowmobile. Things started to fall in place, however, when we remembered a box in Selawik made by Willie Johnson, our first native pastor. He was from Hooper Bay, Alaska, and a very ingenious young man. He used plywood and made a box two feet wide, six feet long, and 20 inches deep and lined it with visqueen, or heavy plastic.

Everyone who knew about it called it Willie's Coffin. It was really nice, because when you have to pack the water up in buckets from the river, it is good to have a small baptismal. You wouldn't want to have a large tank, such as you find in regular church buildings, or you would be all day packing water for it, and then you'd have to warm it up a little. Being baptized in ice water is great, I guess, but most people are not too excited about it.

So it was decided that since we had an airplane we would all go to Selawik and have one service there. Besides most of the six candidates lived there.

Everyone said, "That's a good idea," and they gathered up some old clothes, a change of clothes, maybe jeans and a shirt (they did not need extra shoes) and got ready to go. They love to go anyplace, especially if you'll take them. They are not afraid of flying, they just get in the plane and — go! The pilot does all the worrying.

So on a Wednesday, I asked one of our fine church members in Selawik, Lloyd Davis, to get some water to the sanctuary by hauling it bucket by bucket from the hole in the river ice. This he poured into washtubs on two stoves to warm up, just like the old Saturday night bath. We tried to get the water fairly warm so there would not be too much of a shock.

Martha and I lived in Kotzebue at this time, which is about 90 air miles west of Selawik. If we fly or go by snowmobile we must cross the Hotham Inlet, a river, flat lands, tundra and Selawik Lake. If it is summer and we have to go by water, it is farther. But it was winter and the ceremony would be in Selawik where three candidates lived. The other three lived in Shungnak and Kobuk. Both towns are on the Kobuk River which is about 300 miles long and navigable all the way up.

I made two trips and landed on the village runways that are right at the beach, and picked up the three candidates, and Karl and Molly Geffe, our native minister and his wife, and brought them to Selawik. Then I helped Lloyd by bringing in more water and heating it very hot to pour into the already cooling baptistery.

We had a good crowd, a lot of people came to see what it was like to be baptized. Others came who were sympathetic to us as a church.

We have a lot of people who are sympathetic to Baptists, but they are afraid to be one. A lot of these folks know and believe in the scriptures and the Bible part about baptism, but they still won't do it. Just like folks in the lower 48, you know! Eskimos are no different from anyone else. They have a hard time doing what they know they should do.

It was a wonderful service. We heard some testimonies and just had a good time. Karl baptized the ones from "up river." Then I baptized the ones from Selawik. We didn't have baptismal robes, a choir or anything fancy. We just had a nice curtain we set up in front of the church, and the candidates wore their old clothes. After the ceremony, they wrapped their own blankets around themselves and went to a back room and changed clothes. We had lady attendants for the ladies, but the men didn't get any help. They just had to tough it out.

We said, "OK, go in there," and they said, "OK."

It was sure neat, using a coffin! When we buried them in baptism, we just sat them down in the water and then laid them back and they were buried. All you would have had to do was put a lid on and they would have been sunk. I think to those of us who have had funerals, it was pretty symbolic. Then when they were raised up it was a good symbol of a new resurrection. Our prayers were that they would live the resurrected life.

We went through it really well, and then we all got up and sang some more songs and had a message and that was it. Some people stayed at the church and others stayed with relatives or friends overnight. Most of them have people to stay with. The next day was Friday and I took them home. It was really wonderful and we were pretty happy, even though the service took three days.

Afterwards we emptied the water out by buckets before it froze. We had turned the heat off in the church and it would have been pretty hard to empty a coffin full of ice. We turn the heat off between services as we use oil stoves and it costs too much to keep the buildings warm.

Oil was $140.00 a barrel at that time so was "out of this world" both in price and location. While we were living in Selawik, which we did for four years, we had the heat on in the house section all the time. We had Wednesday night services in the home in winter instead of trying to heat the church. Now, when we have services, someone lights the stove an hour or two before services and it warms up the building.

Now that the baptism was over and the participants and witnesses had gone to their homes, the church building was allowed to cool down until the next service. There were still warm and smiling faces, however, and testimonies of victory and joy.

When Emma was baptized in the promised warm water, she exclaimed, "Ooh!" I knew then that I had failed her and the water was pretty cool. She was a brave soul, however, and allowed me to finish the ceremony.

The Holy Spirit had been filling our fellowship with His fruit as given in Galatians 5:22 and 23, "love, joy, peace, long suffering, gentleness, goodness, faith, meekness, and temperance."

After such a long dry spell in our earlier ministry, and then having six baptisms all at once, we wondered if it was to be the trigger for another outburst of God's saving grace. We were so excited, we could hardly wait to see!

27.

How the Ambler Mission
Got Started

*When James and I would tour the villages, one of our
overnight stops was at Tommy and Clara Lee's home
in Ambler, although the mission was not established
there yet. Tommy had long been interested in Baptist
work and Clara was a strong member of the Friends
Church. These two people and their children were
some of the finest in the village.*

We had visited them and enjoyed their hospitality at various
times for over a year. Usually we would stay overnight and the
next day would travel on to our mission in Shungnak, about 20
miles away. On one occasion, after James and I had had a meeting
in Shungnak and were relaxing in the small living quarters at the
church, we were talking about Tommy and Clara Lee and the
village of Ambler.

James mentioned that Tommy Lee had been wanting to be baptized for the last 5 years. (James and Tommy conversed in Eskimo a lot of the time, and Eskimos don't generally share their deep thoughts with white folks).

I was astonished and asked the obvious question, "Why didn't he mention it?"

James just shrugged the question off as being too difficult to explain.

On our return trip, we of course stopped at Tommy and Clara's again. At this time I talked to Tommy about baptism, and he began to share his ideas about the subject. He also very much wanted a Baptist work in Ambler. Clara said she would be baptized with him, also.

As this was winter and the water was very hard (frozen), we arranged to have the ordinance of baptism in the Kobuk River in front of the village the next summer. All of the villages are located along rivers because they use them for their highways.

The next summer, Martha, James and I flew up to Ambler in our Cessna 170 to baptize Tommy and Clara Lee. We had hoped the villagers would come to the river front to witness this ceremony. Unfortunately, 10 minutes after we landed one of the well-loved old ladies of the village died, and a large number of the town folks went over to the family's house. Consequently, no one joined us at the river except Martha and James and the 7th Day Adventist pastor's wife.

I asked Tommy and Clara to give a short testimony. Tommy's testimony was that 5 years before, he had been thinking and praying about water baptism. One night during this time, he had a dream. He saw a white dove come flying down from heaven and it flew into his body. He evidently related this to Jesus' baptism, where the Holy Spirit, in the form of a dove, rested on Jesus. He took this as a confirmation that he should be baptized.

Clara's testimony was even more amazing. Hers was in two parts. Remember that she had been active in the Friends Church up to this time. She mentioned first of all that some years before

Tommy was saved, she had promised God that if He would save Tommy, she would follow Tommy in whatever he wanted to do.

Secondly, she said that 7 or 8 years before she had a dream that she was in a little Baptist church in Ambler. So, she was willing to be baptized and follow Jesus and Tommy.

This baptism was a special and joyous occasion for all of us. Out of this has grown what we call the "Aquillaq" (Pronounced ak-eel-yak) Baptist Chapel.

For the following two years, I would stop by and have Bible study in their home on a week day, and on Sunday Clara would have a small Sunday School class in her home;

This was our start.

28.

Be Careful in Giving Advice

The pilot of the big Cessna 410 said, "My map shows this airstrip to be 2,500 feet long."

Tony replied, "Yeah, I know the map shows 2,500 feet, but only 1,800 feet of that is usable. The other 700 feet is overrun."

It was 10:00 pm on a dark night in Kobuk, Alaska. Tony Bernhardt, local pilot and guide, and I were standing near the runway after checking our planes for the night. It was in the Fall and we had no snow as yet. The runway was a mixture of gravel and sand and about 1800 feet long with no lights - pitch black! Thirty foot spruce trees were on both sides and at one end of the runway.

We heard a plane flying above us, quite high but seeming to be searching for something. He'd fly off towards the mountains for a ways, and then come back overhead and then fly away again.

Tony and I decided we'd try to contact him by radio and see if we could help. I switched on my aircraft radio to the common frequency of 122.9 and gave a call out into the airwaves. I was rewarded with an immediate response from the pilot. He said he was trying to find the Dahl Creek landing strip over at the foot of the mountains, but as there were no lights, he could not find it.

"How is the condition of your airstrip at Kobuk?" he asked.

Tony and I assumed it was a small light single engine plane, and we told him the airstrip was good. That we had been landing on it.

"OK, do you have any lights down there?"

Tony said, "Tell him I'll light up a can of oil soaked gunny sack material at the beginning end of the runway." In those days we used gallon cans of oil soaked rags for runway markers during emergencies.

"OK, I'm coming in!"

We saw these landing lights coming down out of a black sky. We couldn't even see the plane, it was so dark. There was a great swoosh as this huge 8 or 9 passenger Cessna 410 flashed by us on the landing rollout. He went all the way to the end of the runway before he could get stopped.

After he taxied back and parked the plane in our modest parking area, he shut the engines down and shakily got out of his plane. After introducing ourselves around, he said, "You didn't tell me about the soft spots in the sand. I almost lost control of the plane."

"We had no idea it was such a large plane," we responded. Then the gentleman said, "My map shows this airstrip to be 2,500 feet long, but it seemed awfully short to me." Tony said, "Yeah, I know the map shows 2,500 feet, but only about 1,800 of that is usable, and the other 700 feet is overrun."

We really need to be careful about giving advice before we know all the facts.

29.

Primitive Bible Camps

Every year we would have primitive Bible camps for the kids in the villages. Usually we would have a site on a gravel bar on one of the rivers, such as the Noatak. We would usually have children from two or three villages at each camp.

Being a 'primitive' camp meant we had to carry everything up by boat; food, tents, stoves, appliance fuel, recreational equipment — everything needed had to come up by small boat.

Each year we would fly to Anchorage or Fairbanks and buy about $500.00 worth of food for the camp. That saved us about $500.00 over buying it in Kotzebue. We would buy the food at a market, carry it by car to the airport, stack it in the hanger box by box. When it was time to fly home, we would have the plane loaded to the maximum gross weight and fly to Selawik.

At Selawik, we would unload the plane, box by box, carry the boxes to a boat in the river, run the boat across the river to the church, and store the food there until camp time.

The day before camp was to start, it was all carried back down to the boat, along with all the tents and camping gear. It was then taken to the camp site in several trips and unloaded on the beach.

I mentioned to Martha that by the time we used the food, it was almost worn out. Truly, "Missions in the Arctic is a young man's game."

I once asked Martha, "Why are we doing this?"

And the answer was, "Because no one else is doing it."

We found that 18 or 20 children plus about 6 counselors made a good primitive camp. We have had about 23 camps this far. Praise the Lord!

The kids loved the camps. They got to sleep in tents, help carry water, do their own dishes army style, play, swim and have fun.

We had a pretty regular program, with 2 or 3 summer workers to help. Young men are great for getting driftwood tent poles, putting up tents, helping in cooking, being tent counselors, devotional leaders and taking charge of recreation. We had regular Bible Study, Mission Study, camp fire fun and a message from the camp pastor every night. We had girl counselors also. Especially for the tents. One year we had only boy counselors, and Martha, being the only female present, had to keep peace in two tents of girls. She made sure we had a girl helper the next year.

It was a great time out in the pristine wilderness. After camp was over, the first concern was to get the children home while they were still in good condition. It is a serious business shepherding 20 of someone else's children safely for a week in the woods. All Glory to God! We never had a serious injury or tragic accident in the many camps in various locations we had. Some summers we had 3 camps. It still is a young folk's game. "The strength of youth we lay, at Jesus' feet today......"

30.

God's Tender Care of
His Overwrought Servant

by Martha

*I was so cold and tired I started to cry, and I said,
"Lord, I'm fifty years old! Is this what it's going to
be like the next ten years?"*

The winter of 1979 the airplane was in the shop for repairs,
so in order to do our mission work, we had to go back and use
the snow machine and sled again.

In one month we had gone eleven hundred miles on the snow
machine and sled. And I was so tired of being cold! I was very
discouraged.

It was Saturday and we were on our regular week end trip
from Kotzebue to Selawik and Kiana to minister in the missions.
It was about fifteen degrees below zero Fahrenheit, and as we
traveled we developed a wind that blew back on me and kept me
huddled up and cold.

In the verse of the song, 'Jingle Bells' it mentions 'being up sot'. I always wondered what it meant, and now I know. Every time the sled hit a bump I got upsot! Many times I nearly got thrown out, and I had to settle myself down again. I was so cold and tired I started to cry, and I said, "Lord, I'm 50 years old! Is this what it's going to be like the next ten years?"

When we got to one of the villages on our way to Selawik, Harley stopped and asked if I wanted to stop and warm up awhile. I was so discouraged, I just said, "Let's keep going and get it over with!"

After traveling the one hundred miles from Kotzebue, we arrived at Selawik about 6:30 pm. It was dark and cold. Harley lit the oil stove. We hovered over the stove trying to thaw out.

The next morning we got up and had church services in the mission. After that we ate a small lunch, packed up, and were back on the snow machine and sled. We headed for the Mission in Kiana, about thirty five miles away.

That trip was OK, it only took about two hours and we were in Kiana. We visited in some of the homes and then had services in the church that evening. I was really dreading the eighty mile trip back to Kotzebue that night.

So we packed up and started. I was sitting in the sled, thinking of the long miles in the cold and dreading it.

As we started home we looked up in the sky and saw the most beautiful northern lights we had ever seen. There were many shades of greens and purples, moving and ever changing, brilliant colors, filling the whole sky! Usually northern lights are limited to one section of the sky, not always colorful, and not lasting long. But this night they were all around us, bright and vibrant.

Every once in awhile Harley would drive around in a circle, so I could see the lights that were behind me. These lights lasted all the way home, about four hours.

To me, it was like the Lord had said, "Martha, I do care!"

31.

Getting a Church Building at Ambler

The manager of the phone company in Kotzebue interrupted me and said, "We'll take $500.00. That will be fine."

I did not finish my sentence in which I was going to offer $750.00, up $250.00 from a previous offer. So Aquillaq Baptist Chapel had just bought all the materials for a thirty by forty foot building for only $500.00. Praise the Lord!

From the very start of our mission in Ambler, Tommy and Clara Lee were exemplary church members, and we began planning on how to have a meeting place. We decided to get logs for a foundation from Tommy and Clara's land claim about ten miles up river. The next spring before breakup, we traveled to Tommy's land claim and camped there for a week. There we cut 5 logs and dragged them to the river's edge by snow machine. The plan was to raft them to Ambler after breakup.

That summer Tommy and two of our Southern Baptist summer workers rafted the logs to Ambler. Also, for the last two years there had been pre-cut materials for a 30' X 40' building lying at the side of the airport runway. This was from an abandoned project by the telephone company. They had planned to put a building in Ambler.

Tommy mentioned one day, in passing, that we should try to buy these materials. I said, "Good idea. I'll check on it in the phone company's office in Kotzebue.

I approached the manager in Kotzebue and asked him if they wanted to sell the materials. I said I hadn't really looked at it in detail, but we could probably pay $500.00 for it. He replied, "Well, we'd like to sell it, but we really do not know how much is left there."

I said I would check next week and then talk with him.

When I was in Ambler the following week I looked at the materials more closely and felt a little guilty that I had only offered $500.00. The material and the airfreight to Ambler must have cost them $50,000.00 at least. There were timbers, flooring, siding, doors, plywood, and sheet rock. A lot of the fixtures and accessories had been removed.

When I talked to the manager on my return to Kotzebue, I had it in mind to at least offer $750.00 (We only had $1,000.00 in our checking account). I began my conversation by saying, "I looked at the materials and there are a lot more than I realized and——."

He interrupted me and said. "We'll take $500.00. That will be fine." So I did not complete my sentence in which I was going to offer him the $750.00. So Aquillaq Baptist Chapel had just bought all the materials for a 30' X 40' building for only $500.00. Praise the Lord!

The next summer the California Southern Baptist Brotherhood sent up a volunteer work team and they erected the frame building in about two weeks. In fact, they started on Monday and had church services in the shell the following Sunday. Amen!

This building was divided into two parts, one half for living quarters and one half for a temporary meeting place. Tommy and Clara immediately began having Sunday School in the new building. She is an excellent teacher. In fact, within a few weeks she had twenty-eight enrolled, with an average attendance of twenty one. She had the older children helping her teach the younger ones.

Meanwhile, to get more logs, we had another plan. We would go to Tommy's daughter's land claim, about fifteen miles up river. So the following spring before breakup, my son Danny, myself, Tommy, and Alan Burdick from Kobuk went upriver to Myra's claim and cut about forty logs, about thirty feet long, and dragged them to the river.

That summer Tommy and helpers rafted them down to Ambler and pulled them up to the church site with a Caterpillar tractor.

The following summer, one year later, another work team from California came and put the logs together to make a very nice church building.

32.

Learning to Laugh
Instead of Cry

*"Harley, that crunching noise wasn't your truck tires
on the gravel, it was the sound of crushing something
much more valuable!"*

When we came to the Arctic in 1966 I brought with me one
of my prized possessions, a Gibson Southern Jumbo guitar.
Martha and I purchased it in 1954 shortly after we became
born-again Christians.

This was a used guitar when we bought it, so it was built
when they were largely hand made. At any rate, in November of
1980 the Kotzebue First Baptist Church was hosting the annual
Alaska State Native Baptist Conference. Consequently we had
a lot of visitors and Christian people from all over the state.

This particular day had been quite stormy and by the time
the evening meeting was over at 9:30 pm the wind had risen
above gale force to about 55 knots per hour. At this time we

owned a Cessna 206 airplane, and since it was not headed properly into the wind that afternoon, I asked some of the men to go out to the airport with me and help me turn the plane around.

Several of the men piled into the back of the pickup which had a canopy over it. I put my guitar and case in the back also, and asked them to be careful not to step on it.

The Cessna 206 is quite a heavy airplane and there was a little snow on the ground. We were having trouble pushing it, so I elected to pull the plane with the truck.

The wind was howling and buffeting both the plane and the truck at this point, and it was pitch black, as is usual in the fall. I drove the pickup to the front of the plane, attached the rope to the nose wheel and then to the towing hook on the front of the truck. I did it this way so that while backing up and pulling the plane, I was in a good position to watch what was going on.

What I didn't know was that the men had left the tail gate down when they got out of the truck. I began to back up slowly and in a few feet I heard a crunching noise, like the wheels going through gravel, and so did not think anything of it. I then drove the truck a few feet forward to reposition the truck and through what I again thought was gravel.

I got out of the truck to check the rope and noticed a black object behind the truck. What I had thought was the noise of gravel was my beloved guitar being turned into toothpicks.

What a terrible moment in life! Evidently the wind was blowing so hard it had actually caught the guitar and blown it out of the truck. There was nothing left to do but finish with the airplane and go back to our home.

I walked into our house holding the unbroken neck of the guitar with the strings attached, and a little piece of wood hanging on the strings. As I showed it to Martha, I laughingly said, "Look, this is all that's left of my guitar!"

After I explained the sad story to Martha, she asked me, "Why are you laughing about this? You should be crying."

I said, "I only have two choices, either laugh or cry. I decided I might as well just laugh about it."

It's probably incidents like this that prompted the title of the song "Laughing on the outside, and crying on the inside."

33.

Staying Alive While Learning .

*Some pilots describe small plane flying as hours of
boredom dispersed with moments of sheer terror. In
our early years of flying, the village airstrips in the
Arctic were mostly short and unimproved. These
combined with gusty cross winds, snow and mud at
various times of the year, provided some exciting
landings.*

One of these landings, or attempted landings, was experienced by Martha and me at Selawik while attempting to land our
little Cherokee PA28. This is a low wing, 4-place Piper with
tricycle landing gear. As we approached Selawik during mid-
winter we were faced with an 85 degree 30 knot crosswind. The
runway had been graded, which left snow berms on each side for
the length of the 1800 strip.

The 30 knot cross wind exceeded the little Piper's posted
capabilities somewhat, but I elected to give the landing a try.

Normally, under these conditions the pilot would come in fast with flaps up and attempt to plant the plane on the runway, plop!

However, braking action was very poor, so I decided to try a full stall landing. All went pretty well as we staggered over the threshold, but about 5' above the ground the plane pitched up and down, the nose wheel hit the ground, bounced up, and the plane blew sideways off the runway. There we were, 10' above the snow berms, just above stalling speed, with full throttle, trying to escape the clutches of gravity.

Fortunately the little plane was equal to the occasion, and I was able to turn into the wind and fly to relative safety. I decided to circle over and land on the frozen river that runs through Selawik, which we were able to do. As we taxied the plane to the church and then shut it down and got out, a little boy came running up and said, "You almost crashed, didn't you?"

Martha was delighted to be standing on the ground and I was glad to be alive and still have my plane intact.

34.

Flying to Anchorage the Hard Way

Flying a small plane in Alaska can often be frustrating. The weather plays a large part in the decision of 'to go' — or —'not to go'. Most small planes fly VFR (visual flight rules) because there is so much icing almost the year round.

If there is not actually freezing rain or drizzle on the ground, icing can be found in the clouds. An Instrument rating becomes really valuable for getting in and out of airports and for some en-route white-out conditions that may be encountered.

No one should fly in Alaska, or anywhere for that matter, without enough instrument training to be able to keep the plane under control in case of unavoidable adverse conditions.

It is a lot nicer to fly long distances in Alaska in jets and turbocharged planes, but lots of small planes fly all over Alaska, watching the weather, dodging the weather, and watching the gas gauge.

A major problem encountered in flying from the Arctic to Anchorage, is that we have three different weather systems to contend with: The Arctic weather around Kotzebue, The Yukon Valley weather en route, and the Anchorage Bowl weather at the end of the journey. To make it worse, we have to cross over the Alaska Range, near Denali Mt. (aka Mt. Mckinley). To get over the top one has to climb to an altitude of eight to ten thousand feet. If the ceiling was too low for that I used the long winding Ptarmigan pass which is quite safe. I stay away from the more famous Rainy Pass, as there are too many wrecked planes in there. In other words it is a lot more risky.

Through the years I found my own way to get to Anchorage reasonably safely under low ceilings. One drawback is that it takes about seven hours and is pretty tiring. Also in this kind of weather the anxiety factor is rather high, as you are constantly searching the terrain ahead and deciding whether to go on or turn back.

Add to this the scarcity of air strips and gasoline supplies, and one has to be very careful. It is sometimes about a couple of hundred miles between places where aviation fuel is available.

However, when a person is young and first starting to fly, he or she will do a lot of that kind of flying. When you get older you get tired of it and wait around for better weather, or take the jet!

I finally worked out a route to get to Anchorage if I really had to. It allowed me to fly with ceilings as low as 400' all the way to Windy Pass on the Fairbanks Anchorage highway. I could fly from Kotzebue across the flats, up the Selawik River to its head, through a broad low pass to the Koyukuk River, and follow the river down to Galena. There I would be able to refuel and follow the Yukon River toward Nenana and the highway to Anchorage.

On one particular flight the FAA flight service started advising that VFR flight was not recommended whenever the ceilings were below one thousand feet. This, I think, was to protect them from lawsuits initiated by relatives of foolish pilots who got themselves killed while flying into bad weather even after they had had a briefing. The pilot in command is supposed to make these decisions, but a lawsuit is a lawsuit, and I can't blame the FAA for initiating this warning.

While in Galena on one of these low ceiling flights I called the flight service and asked them for the current weather. They reported the ceilings to be eight hundred feet and ended their briefing by stating that VFR flight was not recommended.

This was the first time I had heard this and it startled me, because the flight service is not expected to give advice, only the weather. I said, "What do you mean VFR flying not recommended? Being from Kotzebue, I think eight hundred feet is a high ceiling for the flat lands."

"Well, we are required to say that," answered the briefer.

I had a little help on this flight from this point on, from the then Catholic priest at Kotzebue, Father Mike Kineike. He is now Bishop of north Alaska. He was at Galena refueling and on his way to Fairbanks. He is an experienced bush pilot and offered to fly up river ahead of me and radio back little reports as we flew.

I followed several miles behind and all went well, although it was a little low at times. As long as I could see the river I wasn't likely to hit a mountain, even with the one mile required visibility. When we got near Nenana, the weather began to clear up, and I was able to continue down the Alaska Highway, through Windy Pass, Summit, Talkeetna, and on to Anchorage. Time en route, seven hours at twelve gallons an hour.

35.

Sled Stories —
Slip

The wreckage was complete. The sled was a broken mess, camping gear was spread all over the river ice. My three red five gallon Jerry jugs of gasoline had rolled the furthest. Sad moment for Harley Shield, pilgrim Arctic traveler.

Traveling by snow machine and sled in Alaska is like other forms of transportation. Mishaps and near disaster can happen at any time, and usually when least expected.

One morning James Hensley and I had packed our sled and were just ready to leave Shungnak for the 12 mile trip up the Kobuk River to the village of Kobuk. Shungnak is situated on a bluff overlooking the river about one hundred feet above the water. In those days there was a path in the center of the village that went straight down the hill. In the springtime, due to some mild thawing and refreezing, this slope could be quite slippery. But as it was shorter than the safe route, we elected to take it.

I was in the lead, and as we approached the top of the hill, we stopped and surveyed the scene. It looked as if we could make it. But at the bottom of the hill, the path went between two oil drums that were about six feet apart. These were solidly frozen into the ground and stood there like sentinels, guarding the trail. Not being an experienced snow machine driver at that time, I figured I could make it all right. James, being more wise in the ways of winter travel and sleds, elected to wait and let me go first.

A couple of ten-year-old boys who attended church and Sunday school were there to see us off. They decided to ride the back runners of my sled down to the river. They said they would try to keep the sled straight. I started down the hill and it was immediately apparent that this was much more slippery than I had thought. It was easy to hold down the speed of the snow machine, but the sled immediately began to slide sideways and catch up. This is what truckers call jack-knifing a trailer.

I increased the speed of the snow machine a little in hopes that I could keep the sled straight. This increased our rate of descent and also made the sled more difficult to manage. I soon was going much faster than I wanted to, and about half way down, I realized we were not going between those two drums in a straight forward manner.

I looked back and saw the sled sliding sideways with the tail end almost up to me, and the boys bailing out, abandoning ship. My last desperate attempt to save the situation was a burst of speed. That was the final straw. The sled rolled almost completely over, sliding on its side with the runners facing downhill. The snow machine was headed straight between the two drums, but the sled hit the drum on the left side and stopped with a crash. The snow machine also stopped and flipped over on its side and I went rolling down onto the river ice and snow. Following, and then passing me were my three five-gallon Jerry jugs, full of gasoline, and several other pieces of camping equipment too numerous to mention.

What a sad moment in the life of this Arctic traveler.

I picked up my snow machine as the gasoline was leaking out of the tank, and began looking over my poor sled. About this time, James, my traveling partner, came up with his snow machine and sled, having wisely gone to the edge of the village and come down the long way to the river's beach. He said, "I was sitting on my snow machine waiting to see you as you came onto the river, because I could not see you as you went over the top of the hill. I finally walked over to the edge of the hill and looked down and saw you spread out all over the river, so came down the other way."

Well, we put my sled on its feet and began to examine it. I had broken one of the runners, five stanchions on one side, and two on the other. The slats that run the length of the sled and carry the load were broken straight across in one place.

We had to unload my sled and carry everything back up to the church building. We relit the fires and pulled the wreckage inside where we could work on it. We were able to get a large roll of heavy nylon fish net cord that is commonly used to lash up sleds, and spent most of the night tying up the broken places. We used tin and stove bolts on the broken runner hoping it would hold together for the rest of the journey.

We were successful enough so that we were able to finish our gospel trip journey to Kobuk and back to Kotzebue without further mishap.

I knew in my mind that I would be making a new sled before the next winter, and so I did.

36.

Sled Stories — Flip

Joe Carter of Noorvik must have wondered about this white man. He had welded his sled hitch for him just fifteen minutes ago and here he was back again asking if he, Joe Carter would mind welding the hitch again.

My first sled was a used dog sled. These sleds were rather narrow and were designed for slow speeds behind dog teams. When we started pulling them behind snow machines, we of course, could travel much faster. Even the early snow machines could pull a sled 20 to 30 miles an hour on a good hard trail. Consequently, they were rather easy to tip over, which I did quite often. My poor wife, Martha, who rode the sled on our travels would get dumped out more often than she liked. Actually, she didn't like it if there was only one upset.

When the sled turned over it strained the sled hitch and sometimes caused it to break.

One time on a trip from Selawik to Kotzebue, when Martha was not with me, James Hensley was following me in another sled. My hitch gave way during the trip, no doubt weakened because of previous mishaps. Pulling the sled with some ropes the last few miles to the village of Noorvik, we stopped at Joe Carter's place. Joe was an old Eskimo man who had a welder. I persuaded Joe to weld my hitch so we continue our trip.

After doing a good job for me, we hooked up and started through Noorvik toward the trail to Kotzebue. While crossing a small lake in the center of the village, I suddenly remembered I had forgotten something at Joe's. Without thinking carefully, I made a sudden U turn on the slippery ice to head back.

The narrow, top heavy sled flipped over and rolled in a complete 360 degree circle, landing upright on its runners. It does not take much imagination to visualize what happened to the newly welded sled hitch.

There was nothing to do but to go back to Joe's and humbly ask him to weld it again. Fortunately he was willing to do this in good spirits and quite gracefully. I suppose old Eskimo men can handle these situations as well as they do because they have traveled so much in the wilds, and have had all sorts of mishaps like this themselves.

37.

A Tragic Weekend

by Martha

This was surely one of the saddest moments in our twenty seven years of married life. One of our boys was gone, drowned in a boating accident. We struggled through the sense of loss that only the death of your own flesh and blood can bring.

In September of 1982, Harley and I went on a family hunting trip. Included in the group were our sons, Larry and Danny, Danny's wife, Mary, and some of their children. Mary's father, Almond Downey, and one of her brothers, Alvin, also accompanied us.

Harley and I had our boat. Danny and all his family were in his boat, and Larry had his 16' aluminum boat. Some of the time Alvin rode in Larry's boat with him.

We had all kinds of weather, good and bad. One night we were in a terrific storm. The wind howled with lots of snow and then rain. The river rose about 15 feet that night. After we went to bed, it snowed so much that it collapsed Larry's little tent, and he had to move in with others.

A few nights later we made our camp as usual. The boats were tied up near by. The next morning the river had gone way down and the boats were high and dry. It took quite awhile to get the big boats back in the water.

This hunting trip lasted 10 days. If I known this I might not have gone. I had thought we would only be gone about 4 days. I thank the Lord for those 10 days, though. He knew what was ahead.

When it came time to go home Larry had trouble with his boat motor. Danny ended up towing Larry's boat back to Noatak village which we had passed on the way back to Kotzebue. We left Larry and Alvin there. The plan was for us to go home. Then Harley would fly one of our motors to the village for Larry to use on his boat, and return home on his own. Larry hadn't gotten a moose yet, so this would give them a chance to hunt on the way.

When we reached Kotzebue we heard there had been a terrible airplane crash in the water, and the son and three year old granddaughter of one of our Kobuk church members had been killed.

A couple from Arizona had come to Kotzebue on a jet to spend a day with us in order to write an article on "A day in the life of the missionaries." We felt it necessary to leave them and go be with the church member in Kobuk on Saturday.

On the way, we flew one of our boat motors up for Larry and Alvin, then on to Kobuk. We stayed several hours in Kobuk and then went back to Kotzebue. We were planning to fly up the river a ways to see if we could spot the boys, but it had gotten so dark as we approached Kotzebue we would not have been able to see them, so dropped the idea.

The next morning as we were getting ready for church, the phone rang. It was Rosaline, Larry's wife. She said that Search and Rescue had been searching the waters for those lost in the airplane crash, and spotted Larry's boat upside down in the water with only Alvin on it. They were searching for Larry.

It was all so unbelievable. All I could say was "No! oh no!" Then I thought of poor Rosaline. We had just celebrated their daughter Christina's second birthday. Another baby was due in January, and Rosie was only twenty three years old.

Harley and the man visiting us got into Harley's plane to fly over the area. I went to the hospital to wait for Rosie and news from Search and Rescue about Larry.

The team brought in Alvin, whose body temperature was so low that they had to work a long time to bring him back to a stable temperature.

But there was no news about Larry. The water at this time of year was ice cold, and there was a 20 knot wind blowing. Hypothermia was almost certain.

Harley came to the hospital and said he was flying overhead when they found Larry, but it did not look good. Rosie came in then and asked if they had found Larry. I said "Yes."

She asked, "Is he OK?"

I had to shake my head and answered "No."

She impulsively cried out, "He won't get to see our baby."

Larry was found face down in ten inches of water. He was almost out of the water. Because of the strong East wind the waters had covered all the sand bars to a depth of about 10 inches. The death certificate says, "Death by drowning," but it was hypothermia that got him.

This was a hard time for us. Losing a child is rough, so different from other family deaths. We had been telling people for years to lean on Jesus. He could really help them through the rough times. Now we needed to live what we had been teaching.

Our immediate family all came for the funeral. We had twelve grandchildren here in Kotzebue. We wanted them to remember Larry alive, so the wife of one of our fellow preachers took care of all the children for us during the funeral.

It took about four hours for the whole funeral including the graveside service.

Family and friends dug the grave ahead of time. Many people helped lower the casket, cover the grave, and lay on the flowers.

A friend of Rosie's made the casket, and the girls and I padded and lined it with powder blue pile. Another friend of theirs made the cross. We all dressed the body after it came back from Anchorage, where it had been taken for an autopsy. This is the way things are done here in the Arctic.

Harley conducted the service and I played the organ. Our youngest son, Tim, had played his guitar and sung a song on cassette ahead of time. It was one that Harley wanted sung at the funeral.

The church was filled; with people even standing around the wall. We sang only songs about heaven and how wonderful it will be up there.

The Lord did sustain us and give us grace and strength to go through this difficult time.

Even now, eight years later as I write this, the hurt is still there. It was hard to write this story, but it shows again how God can meet our every need.

Little Larry Jr. was born the next January. As he is growing up he reminds us so much of his dad.

Alvin told us what happened on the boat that night. Larry had tried to get home. When they came out of the river into the lake, the wind was blowing and the waves were high. The little aluminum boat was heavily loaded and he decided he had better turn back, but as he turned a wave came over the stern and swamped the motor, and it quit. Another wave filled the boat and it capsized.

Larry got on top, but Alvin couldn't. Larry got back into the water and helped Alvin onto the boat, but lost his life jacket which he hadn't put on, but was holding in his hand. He swam after it. The current was too strong to let him get back to the boat. To make it worse, the wind was pushing the boat across the river and away from him. Since it was so dark, he was soon lost from view.

Alvin said he kept calling, "Larry, Larry."

Larry answered, "Stay on the boat!" Alvin had nightmares about this for a long time after the accident.

We do not always understand why God allows some things to happen, but we still believe God is in control, and will work good out of all things.

We have been able to really be of comfort to others who have lost their children. We've been there!

38.

Sled Stories —
How Not To Do It

Everyone is familiar with the nudging of a still small voice inside them when traveling. These little subtle reminders in the subconscious mind are to get them to check what has been done, or something that has been left undone. The inexperienced often ignore these little warnings until they learn that they are valuable tools that will enable them to have a more successful journey.

I can clearly remember my first lesson on this subject in the arctic. It stems from when I first started driving snow machines and pulling sleds on long journeys. We usually fasten our sleds to the snow machine with a metal U shaped hitch called a shackle. It is fastened with a screw type metal pin.

The secret of not losing the sled is to make sure that the screw pin is always tight. Sometimes when we first hook up the sled, we will put the pin in finger tight and then plan to tighten it with a wrench before we leave, easy to forget in the busyness of loading the sled. It is also possible for the pin to loosen while traveling. After a few trips, the driver learns to look back occasionally to see if the sled is still there.

On one of my earlier sled trips I had finished loading the sled and had warmed up the snow machine engine, put on all my warm clothes, and was just ready to start out, when a little voice inside me said, "Are you sure the shackle pin is tight?"

I chose to ignore the nudging, probably saying in my mind, "Oh, it's OK" and began my journey.

About 10 miles later, I looked back to see if the sled was OK, but there was nothing there. I turned around and retraced my trail for about 2 miles before I found the sled, patiently waiting. This seems to be a difficult lesson to learn, but I've found in my 25 years of traveling on snow machines, boats, and airplanes, it is always best to heed these warnings.

We don't always lose sleds because we ignore warnings. Sometimes the hitch will break. Therefore it is wise to look back and check your sled quite often. There are many stories of men who did not practice looking back very often. These people have run their snow machines out of gas, stopped to get more gas from their sled, and discovered their sled was not there. Some have walked as far as 10 miles back to their gasoline supply.

I lost my sled one time on a trip with James Hensley following me. I was driving up on the snow banks of the river, through the willows, looking for Ptarmigan and circling about. I even looked back to see if James was still there a couple of times and never even noticed my sled was gone!

After awhile I stopped just to talk to James, and he pulled up with my sled tied behind his. "Did you lose something?" he asked.

I quickly looked behind my snow machine and realized at last that my sled was not attached to it. I guess my mind was a long way from attending to business that day.

I believe my earlier snow machine days were a lot more exciting because we did not have as good equipment and we had a lot less experience. My first NEW snow machine was a little 1969 12 hp Skidoo. These early machines had bogey wheels and springs for the track suspension. Leaf springs for the skis. On a rough trail they would bounce up and down like a pogo stick, and were hard to control on a rough trail.

I can remember going full throttle with this little snow machine trying to make it up a steep hill while it was pulling a sled loaded with our camping and traveling stuff, along with Martha in the back. I would hit some rough places and start bouncing up and down, then would start tipping from side to side. It would finally bounce so hard it would tip completely on its side, and end up pulling the sled over on its side at the same time. Time to wish for a larger, more stable machine.

39.

Cold Weather Starting

The young Texan preacher had a little white spot appearing on his nose. "Warm your nose with your hand," I told him. "No, not your frozen glove, your warm hand!"

Winter flying in Alaska poses many problems. Especially difficult is the warming and starting of an airplane's engine in the minus 20 to 30 degree temperatures.

One of the more difficult mornings occurred in Shungnak, Alaska during the winter of 1986. I had been in Shungnak with an experienced Alaskan church musician and a young, energetic pastor from Texas. They had come to the Arctic to hold revival meetings in the three villages of the area. We had planned to preach two days in Shungnak, two days in Kobuk, and finish with two days in Ambler.

However, during the time in Shungnak a howling blizzard blew in and descended on us, lasting through the rest of the week.

We were grounded there and spent the days visiting and watching the snow blow by the window. We continued to hold meetings there during the evenings.

I was planning to fly them to Kotzebue on Saturday morning, for they had to catch the Alaska Airlines jet by 4 p.m. to return to Texas.

Friday evening the wind began to die down and Saturday dawned bright, clear and cold. It was thirty-eight degrees below zero. Because of their need to catch the jet in Kotzebue, I decided to go past my limit of thirty degrees below zero for flying small planes. After bundling up and telling the men to come out to the plane in about forty-five minutes, I started out to preheat the engine and hopefully start it.

At this time I had a PA32 Piper, commonly called a Cherokee six, as it is a six place airplane. For heating the engine I use a small propane forced air heater powered with a twelve-volt fan that I hook up to the plane battery. It usually takes about thirty-five to forty-five minutes to warm the engine and oil to enable it to start.

At thirty-eight degrees below zero, a twenty pound tank of propane does not have much pressure, therefore the heater flame was pretty weak and not throwing out much heat. At that temperature, when you first start heating you cannot turn the prop, because the oil is so thick. In fact it is easy to bend a valve push-rod because of the stiffness of the frozen engine. After the engine starts to warm up, you can tell whether the engine is able to start by how easily the propeller will turn.

After what seemed like forever in the cold, I decided to give it a try. So I unhooked the heaters, took off the engine cover and sat on the frozen seat. At this point I need to mention that at these cold temperatures the battery (which is very small in order to keep the weight down) loses about 60% of its power. A person is fortunate to get two attempts to start the engine before the battery goes dead.

I primed the engine copiously, pumped the throttle a few times and pushed the starter button. The starter motor groaned and turned the engine over feebly about two times, and that was all. There was nothing to do but turn off the magnetos and master switch and hook up the heating apparatus again. Now, because of the weak propane pressure, I put the end of the heater right into the cowling and let the weak flame do its best.

By this time the two men had come out, ready to go and found themselves with another hour's wait on their hands. It was a beautiful morning but as cold as all get out. The Alaskan and I were fairly comfortable as long as we kept moving, but the young Texan was getting quite chilled. A little white spot appeared on his nose and we said, "You're getting frost bite, put your hand on the cold spot and warm it."

He didn't want to take his hand out of his warm mitten, so he tried to warm his little frostbite with the cold leather on the outside of his mitten. I said, "No, you have to use your hands!" I put my hand on the exposed area until the white frost was warmed away.

The young Texan was dancing about and getting colder by the minute and said, "I can certainly see that if a person got forced down in this kind of weather, he would have to do everything right in a short time or he might freeze."

I said, "Yes. That's why we carry so much survival gear."

Since the warming process was going to take a little more time, I suggested that the men walk back to a church members house at the end of the runway. There they could have coffee and warm up, while I kept on warming the engine.

I said "I may have this running within another hour, and you'll probably hear the engine and can come out then,"

By this time I was getting kind of cold myself, because I had been out there two hours already, but there was nothing to do but keep on trying, or give it up.

After continuing to heat the engine for another forty five minutes, the engine oil seemed limber enough to warrant trying to start it again. We need to remember, also, that aviation fuel is not as volatile as automotive gas. This is to guard against vapor lock at high altitudes. This has the disadvantage of not wanting to ignite as readily at colder temperatures. One usually has to preheat an engine when the temperature gets below twenty degrees above zero. This makes it doubly important that the carburetor be somewhat warm, thus taking some of the chill from the fuel as it passes through on its way to the engine.

Once again I unhooked all the heating apparatus and crawled into the cockpit and attempted to start the engine. The engine turned over two or three times, fired, turned over two more times and then stopped. That was the end of the battery! There was only one thing left to do, which I hated, and that was to hand prop it, a life threatening situation. Especially when standing on slippery ice and snow. You want to make sure you are falling away from the propeller every time you pull it through, otherwise you might fall into it. Also, a 260 hp engine is no joy to hand prop under the best of conditions.

In the bush, there is no one to call for help. No machinery, no airport service, just you.

After carefully checking everything and priming the engine a couple of times and setting the throttle very carefully at fast idle, I began to hand prop the engine. It actually started quite easily, but died before I could get to the controls. An engine that starts and then dies in cold weather becomes harder to start, because you aren't sure how much to prime it, if at all. If you are not careful you can prime it too much, and soon lose track of whether it needs priming or not.

I had to hand prop for over half an hour before the engine finally started and kept running. This had turned into quite an ordeal. Each time it started, I had to run quickly around the wing and get to the controls before the engine died. I finally made it and kept it running.

I ran the engine for about five minutes and by this time the men had walked out to the plane again. Not wanting to shut the engine off after such a great victory, I left the engine at slow idle and we loaded all the gear into the airplane, being careful not to walk into the spinning propeller. Then we climbed in against the propeller blast of thirty-eight below.

I checked the controls and started to taxi to the runway. At that temperature the windows frosted up so badly that we were constantly scraping the frost from the inside of the windshield. I found that a credit card is one of the best frost scrapers, because it does not scratch the plastic windshield.

At the runway I ran the engine up, and then flexed the constant speed propeller. As the pitch of the propeller changed with the flow of the thick oil flowing through it, it brought the rpm of the engine down, and before I could counteract it, the engine died!

Nothing to do but give it a couple of primes, set the throttle, and hand prop that old 'meat chopper' again. I was relieved to have the engine start rather quickly this second time, and after squeezing everybody back into the plane, we were able to fly a beautiful, uneventful trip back to Kotzebue and catch the jet.

There is one thing about traveling in the bush. You can get in some situations that make you wonder why you ever came to Alaska. But after everything is worked out, and you are comfortably going again, and exulting in the beautiful scenery, you can quote along with Robert Service from the 'Spell of the Yukon', "It's the cussedest land I know, but there's some who'll trade it for none, and I'm one."

That young preacher had some good tales to tell his congregation back in Texas.

40.

Prayer Works

by Martha

Both tanks of the little four place Piper PA28 were showing close to empty. It was dark and Kotzebue was still seventy miles away. We were getting tense.

Harley and I had flown to Dillingham, Alaska to visit our daughter, Lou Ann, and her family. We had a wonderful visit. The day we were to leave, the weather was beautiful, so we took our time leaving.

When we were air borne, it was rather turbulent. I am a smooth weather flyer, so Harley flew higher to get out of the turbulence. It was smooth flying there, but a strong head wind really slowed us down.

We flew and flew but didn't seem to be making much headway. It began to get dark, and we were still a long way from home. It got darker, and then got pitch black. It was pretty lonely up there.

We were still high above the dark clouds and we could not see to get down under them. Kotzebue was reporting clear, so we kept on, knowing we could get clear of the cloud cover before reaching Kotzebue. It was so very dark, that Harley was not exactly sure how far we had come. His instruments showed we were lined up with the course to Kotzebue.

We could hear the radio tower at Kotzebue, but only off and on. We thought we saw the edge of the sound just past Buckland, which is very flat. Harley flew lower, but looking to his left and up, he saw a snow covered mountain, so he quickly went back up.

The village air strip lights are turned on by radio signals from the airplane radio. Harley was flicking the switch for Buckland or Deering hoping to spot the landing strip. One time we saw the lights of the Buckland runway, so Harley turned around to land there, but then the clouds covered the lights and we did not dare try to descend. Nothing to do but proceed on to Kotzebue and hope and pray we wouldn't run out of gasoline.

We were both praying. It was scary! I told the Lord, "You wouldn't want to take us both like this. Think what it would do to our kids."

We finally saw the lights of Kotzebue away off in the distance. By this time the gas tanks were registering empty. Fortunately, there is always a little more in there than the gauge shows. Also, Harley had slowed the plane down to conserve gas. It seemed forever before we landed at the Kotzebue airport and taxied to his plane tie-down place.

What a relief to be back on the ground! I wasn't sure if I ever wanted to fly anywhere again.

The next day I was in charge of a women's group, studying the book, "What Happens When Women Pray?" No one knew what Harley and I had been through the night before. Before I started the study, one of the women said, "I want to share something with you."

She told us that last night she had gotten ready for the women's missionary meeting. She did not know for sure if we were going to have it, but she was ready. She sat down on a chair to wait and fell asleep. She saw "Shields" turning a steering wheel and looking down on one side and then the other.

The Lord woke her up to pray. She did, and then fell asleep again.

The same vision happened again, and she prayed again.

This happened three times and each time the Lord woke her up to pray. The last time she woke, she looked at the clock and saw that it was 9 pm. Her visions and prayers were going on while we were trying to get home. I was amazed! God is so wonderful!

Then I shared our experience of the night before with the women. It was a very impressive and humbling time for all of us. We again realized God's wonderful love and care, and just how important it is that we are faithful and sensitive to the leading of the Spirit in our prayer life.

41.

Sciatica

by Martha

In 1987 around the first part of December, I began to experience quite a bit of pain in my lower back and down the outsides of my legs. I had no idea what had caused the problem, nor what the condition was called.

Out of painful curiosity, I decided to look in my big family medical book to see if I could learn anything. I remembered that Harley had been very uncomfortable driving on our last vacation, due to his wallet in his back pocket pressing on his sciatic nerve.

I found sciatica in the medical book and I surely had all the symptoms. At that time I was regularly going to the public health nurse to have my borderline high blood pressure checked. I casually asked if doctors could do anything for sciatica.

They said, "No." Doctors also tell you to just get lots of bed rest, and if necessary, have back surgery.

One of the workers there in the office said her dad had sciatica and her mother made him go to a chiropractor, and he cured it.

In Kotzebue we have a chiropractor who comes out from Anchorage once a month. He stays for a couple of days each time. Needless to say, I made an appointment with him. He worked on my back both days, working it a little each time. He told me not to sit, but to lie down or stand up, instead.

The chiropractor is a Christian and gives free care to preachers and their families. Again the Lord supplied, and there was no charge for his services.

For about three weeks I was not able to sit much. When I did it was only on a straight backed kitchen chair, and then not for very long. We had our big Christmas family get together with just the Kotzebue family members present, which added up to twenty. I didn't have any trouble cooking and doing all the stand up jobs. It was just the sitting that hurt.

On December 30, my birthday, I had sat down in my normally comfortable rocking chair. I fell asleep. When I woke up I thought, "Oh no! I'll never get out of this chair!" But I did and it didn't hurt.

My sister phoned to wish me a happy birthday and asked how my sciatica was.

I told her, "This is the first day in three weeks that it is not bothering me."

Then I said, "Oh! I know why. This is my birthday and my name is on the Southern Baptist Prayer Calendar. Baptists all over the nation have been praying for me today!" God is faithful to answer the prayers of His children.

I continue to see the chiropractor when my back is bothering me, and he continues to give free service.

Praise the Lord!

42.

Did You See Those Bears?

"I didn't see any bears." I was surprised at son Danny's question.

In the springtime in the arctic, when the days are long, the ice hasn't broken up yet, there is still snow cover, and the mosquitoes haven't awakened, it's nice to go camping for a few days.

One April, I decided to take a few days off and go camp along the upper Hugo Creek, about forty miles north of Kotzebue. My son, Danny, who is always ready to go hunting or do some other outdoor activity, was agreeable to my suggestion that he go out with me and help set up my camp. Then he could return home whenever he wanted.

So it came about that he and I headed out on our snow machines and sleds. Mine was loaded down with tent, wood stove, food, axe, extra gasoline, etc.

After a delightful trip of some three hours in which we traveled up the beautiful Noatak River, (frozen of course), winding through the hills and the spruce trees, we arrived at the desired camp site on the creek.

Danny helped me get the wall tent up and gather some firewood. Since he actually came to hunt for Caribou or look around, he left in the early afternoon. I was content to stay and cut firewood, set up the stove, and generally get the camp in order.

Then I went to the creek and chopped some ice for a water supply. These happy chores consumed three hours or so and I soon had a fire going and hot water on for coffee.

Not long after this I heard Danny's snow machine coming and he appeared at camp with two medium sized black bears he had shot.

The story he had to tell was quite interesting. When he had left me, he traveled up toward the head of the creek and toward the hills of the next drainage. He met four bears coming towards him. Remember this was spring time, and bears were coming out of hibernation. Since Danny was actually looking for Caribou he was only carrying his .17 caliber rifle, which he likes to use because of its flat trajectory and good accuracy. He is a dead shot and can generally place bullets where he wants them, so he elected to shoot a couple of the bears.

He brought one down, but only wounded the second one and it was able to run away. A .17 caliber bullet is not a very heavy projectile for bears but Danny had at it anyway.

Since the first bear lay motionless on the ground, Danny left it for dead and began a two-hour chase after the other one. This chase led him through the forest and the valley and finally on top of a bald mountain, before he was finally able to kill it. He put the bear on his sled and drove all the way back to the first one.

As he drove up, the one he had supposedly killed got shakily to its feet! He immediately shot it again, and it just stood there.

Danny stayed by his snow machine with the motor running in case the bear charged.

Danny was remembering an experience of an Eskimo friend of his. The year before his friend had been driving his snow machine in the same area and came over a hill and saw one of these creatures about two hundred yards away. He turned off his snow machine engine and decided to just sit there and watch him. To his chagrin, the bear immediately charged toward him and the friend desperately began pulling on the starter rope of his snow machine. It wouldn't start.

As the bear came closer, the young man worked faster and just in time the machine started and off he sped. This is why Danny kept the motor running and stood right there as he watched the one that had gotten to its feet. The bear finally gave up the ghost and Danny was able to retrieve the carcass.

When he returned to my camp, he asked me a question, "Did you see those bears behind your tent."

I said, "No, I didn't see any bears."

He said, "Well, I followed the tracks of the other two and they came right down behind your tent. Then they walked around your camp and across the creek."

I went back of my camp and sure enough. There were the foot prints of two bears not fifty feet behind the camp.

We took our snow machines and followed the tracks through the woods and over the hills for quite a ways, and it seemed as if they had kept right on going out of the area.

We went back to camp and I helped Danny prepare the bears for transporting. Danny went back to Kotzebue, leaving me alone with my thoughts, wondering if the bears would return.

Remembering that bears are always hungry and are attracted by smells of food and blood, etc., I took the entrails and things of the two we had cleaned about a half-mile away from camp. I hoped that if they came back they would go over there and leave me alone. That night I slept with my rifle close beside my sleeping bag.

I kept a fire going in the stove and every time a burned piece of wood would fall inside the stove, I would wake up and listen for steps. However, those bears were long gone and I needn't have been so nervous.

This is why during bear season the natives take at least one dog along so they can bark and wake people up when intruders come around.

After that initial introduction, I spent three or four days just enjoying the country. Towards the end of the week, Danny came up to see how I was doing and helped me take camp down, preparatory to going back to Kotzebue.

43.

The Moose That Spoiled
Our Hunting Trip

The moose swam the river right near our tent and calmly walked out on the beach. After he had been duly dispatched with a couple of shots, Coy and I knew we had a lot of work to do.

Towards the middle of September in the Kobuk region of the Arctic, the caribou begin migrating south from the north slope, where they have spent the summer having their calves. It is customary for the Eskimo people to camp along various sections of the Kobuk River in anticipation of the herd's crossing. There they are able to harvest many caribou for their winter's food supply.

Each year about this time, several of our family members spend about a week in the same pursuits of fun and food.

This particular year, my friend Coy Cole and his son-in-law, Randy, came up from Anchorage to go hunting with us. We set out in three boats. My son Danny, his father-in-law and brother-in-law in one boat, Randy and myself in one boat, and my youngest son, Tim, and Coy Cole in Tim's boat. This was kind of a family safari.

We traveled up the Kobuk River about 150 miles from Kotzebue and made camp on the riverbank. Danny and his in-laws had their tent, Coy and I stayed in my tent, and Randy and Tim stayed in Tim's tent.

This type of hunt usually involves two or three days of waiting for the caribou to gather at the river, and be ready for them when they cross the river at some undetermined time. Since there is quite a bit of boat traffic during the day, the caribou are hesitant to move at just any old time. Therefore we have to be ready to jump in the boats when someone cries out, "Caribou are crossing."

Coy and I boated to the other side of the river a mile or so below camp, and walked up in the hills to see if we could find some "camp meat." We didn't have any trouble finding a couple of caribou about 1/2 mile up the hill, and were able to dispatch them quickly.

After cleaning and quartering the animals we began the weary task of carrying the pieces down to the boat. Packing the meat over the tundra and tussocks is a difficult task. This is why Alaskans quickly learn to kill their game as close to the boat as possible. They say they would prefer to have them fall into the boat!

While we were up on the hill we spotted a big herd of caribou about two miles away. So we knew they were getting ready to cross the river at any time. We took our meat back to camp and shared it with the other boys and told them about the herd we saw.

As far as Coy and I were concerned, we were settling down to having a "good camp." We would let the boys go out and run around and hunt all they wanted. We would stay around camp and drink coffee and cook up some meat and enjoy the experience.

Well, the next day, in the late afternoon, someone called out, "Caribou crossing!" and all the lads, including Danny's father-in-law, Almond, climbed into Danny's boat.

"Aren't you coming?" they called to Coy and me.

"No, you go ahead. We'll stay here and take care of the camp," we cheerily replied.

After the boat roared off with the expectant hunters, peaceful silence descended over the camp.

"Ahhh! This is the life," I said to Coy. "Have another cup of coffee. Isn't this a fine hunting trip?"

"Just the way I like it." said Coy as he reached his coffee cup over. The next half hour passed in relative quiet. We talked a little and rested a little, and Coy busied himself fixing some of the meat in preparation for supper.

We were in the tent during this time, and heard an outboard boat coming up the river. As it came even with us the engine stopped. We stepped outside to see who it was. On the far side of the river, which was about three hundred yards wide at this point, we saw a small boat. The boat was between the shore and what appeared to be a large moose swimming toward us. The moose had evidently tried to go back to shore and the Eskimo man in the boat turned him our way.

The moose continued to cross the river and came up on the beach just below our camp. It just stood there. It was a large bull moose with a beautiful rack.

The man in the boat called out and said, "Do you want him? I already have one."

I went in to the tent and got my rifle and said, "I guess we'll have to shoot it, since we're on a hunting trip."

So I aimed for the neck and shot him. The shot went a little low and so did not instantly knock him down. He just stood there and we waited a few moments. The moose had turned away from us, so the second shot would have been difficult. I didn't want to move around too much for fear he would bolt and run off into the woods somewhere and we would have a hard time finding him. The man in the boat had a better angle for a second shot, so he was able hit him in the back bone and the moose fell instantly.

"Well," I said to Coy, "there goes our hunting trip. Now we've got a lot of work to do."

So we began the task of cleaning, skinning and cutting up this tremendous moose that must have easily weighed 1200 pounds on the hoof. We later measured his rack and it was 82 1/2 inches across, which I believe is just inside the trophy class.

It was about three hours later, and had gotten dark, when Coy and I finished cutting up the meat. We were almost exhausted and the hind quarters were so heavy that it took the two of us to drag them up from the edge of the water.

About this time the boys came back, empty handed. They had gone miles up the river, looking and checking, and had found nothing. When they saw this moose, they marveled. Coy's son-in-law was green with envy. He had never killed any large game animal. He kept on saying, "Oh, if I had only stayed in camp! Oh, if I had only stayed in camp!"

Since the meat was on the beach a little ways down river, the next task was to carry it back to camp. I, following in my mother's footsteps, had a bright idea. "Let me bring my boat down and we'll put it on the fore deck."

There was a general muttering of assent from the group such as, "Great!" "Let's try it!" and "Sounds like a good idea to me!"

My little bright idea had not taken into consideration the total weight of the meat, and the rather high free board of the fore deck. However, when the boat was brought to the beach we loaded the meat on. With the boat leaning precariously to one side, and the meat threatening to slide off, I eased the craft along the beach up to the camp. The small lurch that the boat gave when it nosed into the sandy shore was enough to send all the meat sliding into the water.

There was a mixture of cries of dismay and laughter coming from the group of men. This is normal behavior for outdoor men on a camping trip when one of the party goofs.

After a lot more work of washing and rinsing and carrying, we were able to save the meat. I'm sure that during the winter when one of us found a few grains of sand in his moose steak he would remember with amusement my "bright idea".

This type of a camping and hunting trip is pretty typical of an Alaska bush outing.

44.

'Whatsoever He Doeth
Shall Prosper'

"Blessed is the man that walketh not in the council
of the ungodly, nor standeth in the way of sinners,
nor sitteth in the seat of the scornful. But his delight
is in the law of the Lord; and in his law doth he
meditate day and night. And he shall be like a tree
planted by the rivers of water, that bringeth forth his
fruit in his season; his leaf also shall not wither; and
whatsoever he doeth shall prosper." Psalm 1: 1 - 3

In chapter 3, "Going to Bible School", we gave an account
of our sincere desire to live by the Bible as much as possible, and
to test its promises by attending Multnomah on faith alone.

Now, thirty-five years later, and through all of our experiences, we have proved "Experiential Christianity" works. In
other words, the Bible means what it says.

In all these years, we have never gone hungry, except when too busy in the work to eat regularly. God gave us six beautiful, intelligent children. All our health has been excellent. Our medical bills averaged only $20.00 a year through the child raising years, and very little more since.

God has used us in Hoopa and in the Arctic in starting churches and missions, leading many to salvation by faith in our Lord Jesus Christ.

We have influenced others through preaching, Bible studies, and area mission conferences. We have encouraged, instructed, and sometimes rebuked through personal visitation.

We have ministered to countless numbers of children through Sunday Schools, vacation Bible schools, summer camps, and boys and girls clubs and activities.

Through it all we have tried to maintain an evangelistic thread that presents Jesus Christ as Lord and Savior of our lives, and to lead those who come across our path to receive Him in their hearts.

As you read these pages, we hope that you have caught a glimpse of God's faithfulness to those who "Wholly follow the Lord." It is our desire that each of you will catch the flame of missions.

The world may think you are a fool if you seemingly throw your life away in a place like the Arctic, but as Paul so aptly put it in 1 Corinthians 4:10, "We are fools for Christ's sake."

Like the book of Acts, this book is not yet ended, as we continue to minister in the Arctic through our retirement years.

finis

In the year of our Lord, 1998

Information About the Writers

Harley D. Shield — Decided to follow Jesus in 1954; has BA in Education, and Special Secondary Industrial Arts Teaching Credential at San Jose State College; took one-year graduate course in Multnomah School of the Bible in Portland, OR; received General Elementary Teaching Credential at Humboldt State in Arcata, CA; Master of Divinity degree at Golden Gate Baptist Theological Seminary; taught high school and elementary school four years; and has been a missionary thirty-five years.

Martha J. Shield — Accepted and started following Christ in 1954; graduated from South San Francisco High School; Attended University of California at Santa Barbara; quit the university to get married; has been a wife, mother and missionary ever since. Also, for many years, in Kotzebue Alaska, she owned and operated the world's smallest and most northerly Bible Book Store, "The Sonshine Book Store".

Illustrator Darlene Thiesies invited Christ into her life in 1948. She has received a National Art Scholarship and numerous awards. She is self-taught in many mediums and sells paintings in galleries. Since 1968 she has been teaching all ages, and her outreach ministries in chalk and black light art Evangelism are very popular.

Compiler Jan M. Overholser — Accepted Christ as Savior in 1930; has BS in Education from Western Oregon University; taught elementary school nineteen years; past president of Oregon Christian Writers; past editor of Oregon Flying Farmer news; has written editorials and articles for several newspapers and magazines; currently a newspaper correspondent.

Order Information

To order additional copies of
Loud Singer and Little Bird,
send $12.95 plus
$2.00 shipping and handling
per book to:

Arctic Publications
Harley D. Shield
928 Kokomo Street
Fairbanks, Alaska 99712